Education for the twenty-first century

Hedley Beare and Richard Slaughter

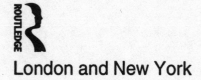

London and New York

First published 1993
by Routledge
11 New Fetter Lane, London EC4P 4EE

Simultaneously published in the USA and Canada
by Routledge
29 West 35th Street, New York, NY 10001

Reprinted 1993

First published in paperback in 1994

© 1993 Hedley Beare and Richard Slaughter

Typeset by LaserScript, Mitcham, Surrey
Printed and bound in Great Britain by
Mackays of Chatham PLC, Chatham, Kent

British Library Cataloguing in Publication Data

A catalogue record for this book is available from the British Library

Library of Congress Cataloging in Publication Data.

A catalog record for this book has been requested

ISBN 0–415–11523–X

Education for the twenty-first century (Bea)

This book has grown out of a common and deep-seated concern, at a time when many educators are worried about some of the trendlines in school reform, about the way young people think of their own future, and about some of the relatively simplistic education reforms being advocated, often by people with scant comprehension of modern educational practices. Schools as institutions, schooling patterns, the curriculum and teachers themselves have come under heavy criticism throughout the past decade, but it now has to be recognised that the problems in education have no lasting or satisfactory solutions while schools continue to operate out of the framework which has determined their *raison d'être* for the past two hundred years. The authors argue that schools do not need fine tuning, or more of the same; rather some of the fundamental assumptions about schooling have to be revised. They argue that learning about the future must become very much a part of the present, and they set out in the book some of the thinking and several techniques which permit us to confront the future and to make it a more friendly place. The first part of the book explores three of the macro-changes taking a foothold in people's thinking across the world: the post-industrial economy and the consequences of unrestrained industrialisation; global consciousness and concerns about the environment; the ways of knowledge production and the limitations of scientific materialism as the 'one best way'. The second part suggests techniques, practical approaches and direct action which permit constructive educational responses to these macro-changes.

Professor Hedley Beare and **Dr Richard Slaughter** are members of the Department of Policy, Context and Evaluation Studies in the University of Melbourne's Institute of Education.

Educational management series

Series editor: Cyril Poster

He looked around him as if seeing the world for the first time. The world was beautiful, strange and mysterious. Here was blue, here was yellow, here was green, sky and river, woods and mountains, all beautiful, all mysterious and enchanting, and in the midst of it, he, Siddhartha, the awakened one, on the way to himself. All this, all this yellow and blue, river and wood, passed for the first time across Siddhartha's eyes. It was no longer the magic of Mara, it was no more the veil of Maya, it was no longer meaningless and the chance diversities of the appearances of the world, despised by deep-thinking Brahmins, who scorned diversity, who sought unity. River was river, and if the One and the Divine in Siddhartha secretly lived in blue and river, it was just the divine art and intention that there should be yellow and blue, there sky and wood – and here Siddhartha. *Meaning and reality were not hidden somewhere behind things, they were in them, in all of them.*

Hermann Hesse, *Siddhartha*, 1951 (Emphasis added)

Formerly the future was given to us; now it must be achieved.

Jonathan Schell, *The Fate of the Earth*, 1982

Contents

Figures

Foreword

Education for the twenty-first century is a lively and forceful book which should encourage passionate debate about the future, where schools are going and what the syllabus should include. As the authors say: 'Most of the writing, planning and public debate about education assumes a fairly static world picture'.

Australia is moving into an unknown future with an unparalleled complexity of options open to us. We advance into a strange landscape, without maps or sign posts. Hedley Beare and Rick Slaughter are sensible, well-qualified and adventurous guides for the future. Their book is both practical and imaginative.

To mix metaphors, Australians have been sprinters rather than marathoners, reluctant to plan for the medium to long term. We are paying a heavy price for our failure to confront global, long-term issues in a time of technological revolution.

Is our education system capable of bearing the weight we will need to place on it? A century ago, schools might probably have provided about 40 per cent of all the information about the world that young people received, reinforced by contact, in and out of class, with the peer group. Home and church/Sunday school would have had more collective input than books or newspapers.

Schools once set the information agenda, although that term was not used, while home and church set the moral agenda. Now the cultural agenda is set electronically. Schools and even homes seem to have become part of the counter-culture, the resistance, fighting back with a declining share of the action.

There is a widening gap between classroom experience, which is often static and boring, where rigour and rigidity have been confused, and electronic media which tend to be non-demanding, variegated and aimed at instant gratification. In the 1960s television was welcomed as a major force for education and stimulation. How has it worked out in practice? Education never knew what hit it. Schools have rapidly declined as formative influences. Tough subjects such as the sciences, mathematics and languages are falling sharply.

There is much in the book that I disagree with – but in a way that adds to its appeal. It stimulates fresh thought. Reading the book forced me to rethink many of my own ideas (or prejudices) and that in itself makes it worth close study.

Barry O. Jones
(former Minister for Science,
Parliament of Australia and
National President of the
Australian Labor Party)

Acknowledgements

The authors would like to thank the following publishers for permission to use quotations from the following works:

Herman Hesse, *Siddhartha*, 1951. New Directions Publishing Corporation, New York. Jonathan Schell, *The Fate of the Earth*, 1982. Jonathan Cape, London. G. Brundtland, (*et al.*), *Our Common Future*, 1987. Oxford University Press. Lewis Mumford, *The Pentagon Power*, 1971. Martin Secker & Warburg, London. Willis Harman, *Global Mind Change*, 1988. Warner Books, New York. Walter Anderson, *To Govern Evolution*, 1987. Harcourt Brace Jovanovich, London. Larry Dossey, Space, Time and Medicine. Shambhala Publications, Inc., Boulder and London, William Leiss, *The Limits to Satisfaction*, 1976. University of Toronto Press, Fraser, J. T. *Time the Familiar Stranger*, 1987. Tempus Books, Microsoft Corporation, Washington D.C. Drexler, K. Engines of Creation, 1986. Anchor/Doubleday, New York. Robert Fitch and Cordell Svengalis, *Futures Unlimited: Teaching About Worlds to Come*, 1979. National Council for the Social Studies, Washington D.C. Elise Boulding, *The Dynamics of Imaging Futures*, 1978. World Future Society Bulletin, Bethesda, MD. Joel Kovel, *Against the State of Nuclear Terror*, 1983. Central Independent Television, Birmingham, UK. Wilber, K. *Up From Eden*, 1983. Routledge and Kegan Paul, London.

Introduction
How this book came to be

This book grew out of a common and deep-seated concern. As colleagues on the same faculty, we discovered that we were both using parallel and complementary materials while caught up in a flurry of talks, speeches, and workshops with educators who were worried about some of the trendlines in school reform, about the way young people think of their own future, and about some of the relatively simplistic educational reforms being advocated, often by people with scant comprehension of modern educational practices. Schools as institutions, schooling patterns, the curriculum and teachers were criticised, quite trenchantly and unfairly at times, throughout the 1980s, to such an extent in fact that the reform agenda appeared to have been taken out of the hands of the providers. Economic factors and how 'useful' education is – instrumentalism, it has been called – seemed to be driving the reformers, especially the policy makers and the politicians.

Schools were in the same no-win situation in which Brer Rabbit found himself in Uncle Remus's story about the Tar Baby; the more Brer Rabbit punched and kicked, the more he stuck to the tar baby. The problems in education, we now realise, have no lasting or satisfactory solutions while schools operate out of the framework which has determined their *raison d'être* for the past two hundred years. Education does not need fine-tuning, or more of the same; rather the fundamental assumptions about schools have to be revised. That may sound an awesome diagnosis – and of course it is – except that teachers are perennial optimists, incorrigible innovators, and they make qualitative improvements in every working day as they prepare and present their learning programmes. For a group so consistently maligned and made scapegoats for societal failures, they show remarkable altruism, commitment, resilience, and above all understanding. Clearly, schools are already doing something about the twenty-first century. It only requires some clearer vision, a stronger sense of direction, and some consistency in the way teachers operate to effect wholesale transformations.

We were aware that world-views are changing, fast and dramatically; the events during the early 1990s in the former Soviet Union, in South Africa, in the European Community, in Asia are evidence of how fundamental assumptions are being reworked. Just as Zero Population Growth (ZPG) became accepted rapidly across the globe in the late 1970s and early 1980s and began to show up in birthrate figures within half a decade, so there are several other ideas which will radically alter the world in the next few years because they are becoming widely accepted as the basis for the ordinary person's daily behaviours. The global ecology – care for the planet – is one such notion which we deal with in chapter 3.

We know that 'time is running out', that there are cultural lags, that the poorly educated are sometimes among the world's worst polluters, that the 'here-and-now' still takes precedence over 'the extended present', and so on; but we can still do something about it. Furthermore, individual students, teachers, and parents can be part of the action. So we set out in this book to empower them, to put into the hands of these key people some of the thinking and the techniques which permit us to confront the future and to make it a more friendly place.

The materials in this book have been used in a number of workshops largely involving senior teachers and school administrators. Over a period of time this process not only refines the materials but also allows them to be couched in language which renders them more accessible and useable. In short, the book's contents have been road-tested. These materials have also been used in articles and papers. Here we have tried to synthesise these materials in a form which teachers, parents, and, we hope, students can readily use.

By its nature, much of the content of this book is at base complex, and it is frequently available only in out-of-the-way publications – though that is becoming less so. We have attempted throughout to use simple language, to be luminous, to avoid obscurantist argument; we have tried to be readable and immediately comprehensible. To be thus, one has to pay a price, and we are aware that there are important qualifications which we have had to overlook in some of our chapters. Two require comment.

We know that we seem to be addressing Western cultures throughout the book. We are aware of the impact of other cultures and of the fact that they may well save the world community by sponsoring better assumptions, more defensible behaviours, more ennobling attitudes, more cohesive visions. Even so, the Western world-view has had such a world-wide impact and has been taken for granted for so long that we felt compelled to concentrate on its consequences.

We are also aware of the limitations of the hierarchy metaphor, especially as we have addressed it in chapter 4 and beyond. There are of course dangers in setting things in hierarchies, for they tend to reify both dominance and domination, they lead to the false logic that higher automatically means better, and they are unidimensional. We much prefer metaphors about connections and networks, about overlapping sets, about integration and harmonising. Our materials in part governed our approaches here, for we were trying to make accessible some of the thinking which has led to the more embracing paradigm.

Apart from the Introduction and the reprise (i.e., the Conclusion), the symphony we play here has two major movements. In chapters 2, 3 and 4 we deal with three of the macro-changes taking a foothold in people's thinking across the world; taken seriously and acted upon, these ideas will change the world, literally. In the following chapters we suggest techniques, practical approaches, and direct action which derive from those macro-changes. In answer to the question, 'But what can we *do*?' we aimed to give some practical answers.

We are grateful for the help of many people in compiling this work. A book like this has the habit of invading our lives, sitting with us at breakfast, intruding into our household conversations, forcing forbearance on our family and close friends. We are in debt to our spouses and long-suffering close associates. No one has been more central to the success of this venture than Ms Trudy Lingwood, whose remarkable skills as an organiser and on the keyboard have saved us the marginal hours which made it possible to bring this book into being. Finally we would like to thank the Hon. Barry Jones both for his valuable Foreword, and for the many helpful comments on the text.

Hedley Beare
Richard Slaughter
Institute of Education
University of Melbourne

Chapter 1

The dimensions of change

Over the course of this century, the relationship between the human world and the planet that sustains it has undergone a profound change.

When the century began, neither the human numbers nor technology had the power radically to alter planetary systems. As the century closes, not only do vastly increased human numbers and their activities have that power, but major unintended changes are occurring in the atmosphere, in soils, in waters, among plants and animals, and in the relationships between these. The rate of change is outstripping the ability of scientific disciplines and our current capabilities to assess and advise. It is frustrating the attempts of political and economic institutions, which evolved in a different, more fragmented world, to adapt and cope.

G. Brundtland *et al.*, *Our Common Future*, 1987

Most of the writing, planning and public debate about education assumes a fairly static world-picture. Schools, students, the curriculum, classrooms, teachers, and the policies and functions of educational systems are treated as though these have been, are, and will continue to be enduring features of education, wherever we are in the world. Yet the universe is anything but static and its dynamism poses quite powerful challenges to educators. Moreover, the fundamental assumptions which govern our thinking about educational systems are themselves derived from a set of dominant, but often unexamined, assumptions about the nature of the world. They concern such things as growth, economic rationality and the separation of people from nature. They are based, in fact, on a world-view from before the Industrial Revolution.

But in many key respects that world-view is being exploded by quantum physics, by technology, and by planetary pollution as well as by social innovations such as the 'theology of ecology', the 'green movement' and ideas like the 're-enchantment of the world'. What have been called 'structural discontinuities' (that is, breaks in the social fabric based on the 'cultural programming' of an earlier time) certainly complicate the work of teachers and schools. If schools are to operate confidently in the twenty-first century, these issues need to be understood *now*, especially by teachers and parents.

This book tries to show how educators and people associated with schools can respond to these challenges. The response implies a journey which goes far beyond the present familiar landscape of schooling, and beyond the easy acceptance of what we now take for granted about education. In fact, it is that very taken-for-granted-ness which is the fundamental problem. In chapters 2, 3, and 4, we therefore draw attention to major world changes occurring before our eyes and, more importantly, to the shifts in world-view which are driving them.

The central importance of changes in values, in ways of knowing, in assumptions about meanings – in short, the implication of paradigm shifts – has too often been overlooked in educational discourse. However, understanding these deep-seated changes opens up many new options. While it is impossible to predict the future accurately (and especially the future of social systems), we attempt here what may be the next best thing: a specifically forward-looking educational perspective which can help us to re-conceptualise what education for the twenty-first century could be. Using what we presently know, accepting some of the more obvious trendlines, and without slipping into the predictive mode, we can already consider a number of things which will occur in the next decade or century.

CHANGES THAT ARE LIKELY TO OCCUR

The first thing to note is that the changes of the next one hundred years are likely to exceed those of the last one thousand years in terms of impact, speed, scope and importance. For example, within the next century we are likely to see some or most of these events:

- A doubling of the human life span. Think of the consequences such a development will have on social structures, on family life, on promotion in one's employment, on the meaning of work and of retirement.
- The successful completion of the human genome project and a blurring of the boundaries between human beings and machines. Ethical dilemmas are already occurring in relation to genetic engineering, *in vitro* fertilization, transplantation of human organs and organ banks. Such developments will continue to require the rewriting of laws, the reframing of ethical concepts and a redefinition of life and consciousness.
- The loss of most of the world's remaining tropical forests. This one development will greatly deplete the planet's evolutionary gene pool and will hasten climatic changes across the globe.
- An exacerbation of the greenhouse effect coupled with further ozone depletion. Thus skin cancer will become more prevalent and there will be a range of other impacts on plants, animals and environments.
- The development of nanotechnology: tiny machines or 'replicating assemblers' working at the molecular level to fabricate sophisticated materials and construct devices of enormous power at very low cost. If this technology lives up to its promise it will overturn economic systems, transform the natural and built environments, revolutionize health care, defence and space travel.
- Conventional and nuclear terrorism may well worsen. In consequence, our present notions about security, mass travel, and national borders are likely to change. The spread of the AIDS pandemic will exacerbate these concerns.
- The sovereign nation-state may decline in power. What we now take for granted about world politics, about nations and government, about who makes decisions for our collective good will all have to be rethought.

To such a list could be added new forms of 'learning' via chemical or electronic implants, inter-species communication, genetic counselling and many other shifts, social innovations and new types of technology (including nuclear fusion, expert systems and space manufacturing). The combined effects of such changes are powerful, bewildering, and essentially unpredictable. For as far ahead as we can see, there will be turbulence and deep-seated, structural change. While we may yearn for more settled times, they are not likely to reappear, at least for a very long time (in human terms). So what are the consequences for schooling and for what children now in school should learn?

No picture of the future can possibly be complete. These things will not all happen in ways we might expect. There will be many surprises! But some of them are very likely to occur simply because their precursors (or early warning signs) are already here. So without looking far into the future and without having to try very hard, we can see major changes happening right before our eyes. Taken together, they are altering some of the most basic assumptions about, and conditions of, life on planet Earth. Of all the institutions in society, of course, schools must be among the first to address these issues, if only because the students now in school will live amongst these changes. What is more, to educate young people as though the present patterns of thinking and living, or past ones for that matter, provide a sound basis for confronting the future is quite plainly dangerous. No curriculum can afford to overlook this prospect.

We are, in other words, at a major historical divide. Many writers and commentators have been making this point for several decades. This transition away from what we have taken for granted affects the viability of all institutions and the life of every individual. Yet, curiously, there is little evidence that those who are running schools and school systems are aware of the implications of these rapid, fundamental, and structural changes. In fact, the futures-related tools and techniques which have been developed and applied in other contexts for more than forty years are simply not part of the standard equipment of teachers or of school administration, of educational policy-making or of parent participation in their children's education. With a little effort, they could be.

This book is therefore an attempt to put some of these materials in a form which can be used by educators, and to help people to come to terms with the necessary changes to the framework out of which we interpret education, and indeed our world. If educators in particular could supersede the industrial worldview, if they could be encouraged to take an active and sustained interest in the broad span of futures now confronting us, and if this awareness were considered a necessary part of the professional knowledge of educators, then our society, its institutions, and especially its schools would begin to look and function very differently.

THE 'DEFAULT FUTURE'

So where do we start? Where better than with our common, default notion of the future? It is clear that 'the future' is generally regarded as a background abstraction which serves only to frame our plans and intentions over the next few hours, days, weeks or years. In other words, it acts as a kind of blank screen upon which to project our hopes and fears. Viewed from within an industrial framework it lacks substance and reality. Even these minimal uses tend to be informal and short-term. However, some people, including a number of large organisations, have found it necessary to take a longer view in order to improve their planning, or because there are long lead-times involved in major projects. This provides a clue to the real importance of the futures dimension.

Even so, the collective investment in futures study and futures research is pretty minimal. Is this because we know that we will not be around to see the results? If so, what about our children? Is it not rather odd that on the one hand we are collectively causing and then maintaining powerful and revolutionary waves of change which extend far into the future while, on the other hand, we restrict our attention to our known past or the short-term present?

The common practice of minimising any consideration of futures-related concerns has been called 'future discounting'. It leads us to underestimate the importance of alternatives, choices or consequences. Various metaphors have been used to describe future discounting. For example, our society has been likened to a vehicle powered by the forward motion of time and equipped with many comforts and diversions, but lacking either a navigator or maps. To extend the metaphor in the way McLuhan did, we are so used to driving with our eyes fixed on the rear-vision mirror that we overlook where we are going, or why we have undertaken the journey.

So what can we say about where the planet and all the creatures on it are going? This is a crucial question to confront, for it affects everything the education process stands for. A balanced reading of contemporary evidence across a number of fields suggests that we are accumulating a wide range of very serious problems which will certainly restrict the choices available to later generations. Naive optimists argue that human ingenuity and continuing techno-logical innovation will keep us ahead of any calamity, but it is abundantly clear that the very success of our species has brought it to the point where it has put its own survival in question.

This is why the big picture is so important and also why we need a better appreciation of what might be meant by 'the future'. Some things may make perfect sense when they are considered at close range and in isolation, but when they are reconnected to the broad processes of social, economic, technical and environmental change, we can see the human race steadily painting itself into a dangerous corner. Industrialised cultures have gone for short-term exploitation and profit, leaving future generations to foot the bill. However, important as these issues are, it is a mistake to focus exclusively upon the external manifestations of the threat. Repeatedly discussing 'world problems' and 'solutions' out of a non-critical framework, although well-intended, can miss the essential point.

LIMITATIONS OF THE INDUSTRIAL WORLD-VIEW

So what is the essential point which we appear to be overlooking? Perhaps the key proposition of this book is this: it is impossible to confront the great global or educational issues of our time without also considering the frameworks of meaning and value which brought them into being in the first place.

This proposition can be clarified through the architectural metaphor given in Figure 1.1. Here the artist has drawn a parallel between physical architecture and social architecture. The former has a superstructure comprising all the familiar elements (like buildings, streets, signs), an underlying framework (foundations), and a site upon which the whole complex rests. Similarly, the social structure (comprising elements like language, symbols, customs, laws) rests upon a hidden structure of norms, assumptions, ethical and moral commitments which themselves stand or fall on the epistemological foundations of a world-view or paradigm. This set of analogies makes it abundantly clear why superficial analyses often fail; they only consider the structures sitting on the surface.

A profound change seems to be occurring in the way we perceive ourselves and the earth we inhabit; indeed, the change reached flood proportions during the late 1980s. A spate of books and writings which appeared during that decade, when taken together, steadily revealed the outlines of a renewed world-view. Many of them drew upon the ground-breaking work of Thomas Kuhn in his book *The Structure of Scientific Revolutions* (1962). Kuhn showed how the work of scientists was structured by a shared set of

The architectural metaphor

SCOPE OF ENVIRONMENT DESIGN / CULTURE DESIGN

SOCIAL ARCHITECTURE

SOCIAL STRUCTURE
Language/symbols, customs laws, constitutions, institutions

UNDERLYING STRUCTURE
Cultural norms/assumptions
Ethical/moral framework

WORLD VIEW / PARADIGM
Understanding of reality, nature/human nature

PHYSICAL ARCHITECTURE

SUPERSTRUCTURE
buildings, streets, signs, walls, doors, windows

UNDERLYING FRAMEWORK
Footings/substructure

SITE / FOUNDATION
clay, sand, rock, water

SUPREME COURT

NEW WORLD AIRLINES

POLICE

NO STANDING

STATE G... COMMI...

Figure 1.1 The architectural metaphor

assumptions about how reality is defined and organised. A disciplinary paradigm, as he called it, supplied a context within which people worked, often unaware of its shaping influence upon their perceptions and work. For much of the time people engaged in routine puzzle solving – that is until problems accumulated that could not be resolved in the current paradigm. There then followed a period of radical uncertainty, or revolutionary science when the whole structure was laid open for change. The wider appeal of these ideas is obvious and the attempt to construct a new cultural paradigm has proceeded apace.

One person who helped to popularise the transformation was Marilyn Ferguson. As a journalist and author researching materials for her writings during the 1970s, she became aware of several major intellectual shifts which seemed to be occurring across a range of disciplines, and which she tried to document in her book *The Aquarian Conspiracy* (1980). In the fields of medicine, education, the social sciences, economics, government, psychology, religion and politics, she was struck by the fact that there seemed to be a high degree of consistency in what was evolving simultaneously. She called it 'the whole-earth conspiracy', a 'startling worldview that gathers into its framework breakthrough science and insights from earliest recorded thought' (Ferguson, 1980: 23).

She became convinced that a paradigm shift was taking place, producing a context within which people 'found themselves re-thinking everything' (ibid.: 24). The Catholic scientist-priest Teilhard de Chardin was a constant source of insight, she found, and was being often quoted; it was he who said that 'the future . . . is in the hands of those who can give tomorrow's generations valid reasons to live and hope' (ibid.: 43). Though his reputation has waxed and waned, it was also Teilhard who coined the term 'cosmogenesis' to indicate that new ideas were being generated about how the world was formed. Teilhard tried to synthesise both the religious and the scientific myths about the creation of this planet and the galaxies. He suggested that human beings, as one of the species on planet Earth, were capable of 'continuous transformation and transcendence' (ibid.: 29). The new perspective, Ferguson observed, was about 'the ecology of everything', about connectedness, about what has been termed the 'everything-hangs-together' philosophy.

Viewed now, more than a decade later, Ferguson's book appears incomplete, flawed, in places naive and tentative, and often unsatisfying in that it stops short at the edge of darkness, not venturing into the void. Exploratory books tend to be like that. There are of course dimensions to physics and cosmology, astronomy, mathematics, medicine, genetic engineering, space science and so on which are well beyond the understanding of any one person, and the temptation is to pull back and leave these areas alone. But every new theory, new venture or new invention has aspects which its initiator knows nothing about. The whole point of exploration is that the explorer is in unknown territory for which there is no reliable map to travel by. Ferguson's book suffers from some of these defects, and in consequence it helped to spawn some silly New Age developments as well as some profound questionings. Most important for our purposes here, however, is that she helped us to be more specific about what the paradigm shift entails.

In the chapters which follow, we suggest that discussions of world problems are inadequate if they do not consider the epistemological foundations on which the problem is predicated. The world is a highly structured, interconnected system, a number of whose features or qualities are obscured from us by the limitations of the dominant mode of rationality which flows from the scientific/industrial world-view. All of us, in other words, consistently simplify our view of the world in a way which frustrates our attempts to achieve a coherent grasp of its problems. So we invent the familiar litany of global problems, the so-called *problèmes globales*, without being able to conceive of a way of solving them.

In fact, the mode of consciousness which has become 'normal' over the last two centuries contains its own contradictions. One is that, because it is focused upon the here and now, the not-here and the not-now have come to seem remote and unreal. Yet to be alive is to participate deeply in a web of interactions embracing past, present and future. If this participation were experienced as a reality, we would conceive of our relationship to the environment and its web of life in an entirely different way. But we have inherited a short-sighted and self-centred view which is obsessed with power over nature rather than participation in it.

This diminished view about reality is of relatively recent origin, but the consequences of being so self-assured over the centuries have become the stuff of myth and legend. They recall the classical concept of *hubris*, or contemptuous, unjustified pride, and the unfortunate price paid for it is *nemesis*, or destruction – a fact already well understood by the collective unconscious. It is therefore consistent that one of the distinguishing features of the twentieth century has been the outpouring of apocalyptic imagery in literature, art, film, and the mass media. Literal 'hells on earth' have become fully imaginable (many would say likely) because Western cultures, mediated through the systematic distortion of inadequate belief-systems, create their pre-conditions every day. But it does not have to be this way: futures can be envisaged which lead in other directions. That is the major message of this book.

To put the matter briefly, the Western/industrial world-view based on certainty, predictability, control and instrumental rationality (i.e. reason applied to unquestioned practical ends) has become fractured and incoherent. Many core values and beliefs which once sustained the social fabric have decayed and are perceived as empty, threatening, problematic. The results are there for all to see. Some people like to preach about moral decline and the loss of standards, but the problem is much deeper than that, for the world-view which sustains that argument is itself coming apart in an historically unprecedented way. The planet supports over five billion people, some of whom are equipped with world-shaping, or world-destroying, technologies. In addition, many of the less fortunate are destroying whole ecosystems simply to survive. The single most notable consequence of the industrial era may be that the planet's capacity to support life is being steadily eroded.

The current frame of reference had its origins about three hundred years ago when, with the age of scientific enlightenment, the ideas of Isaac Newton and René Descartes became fused, constructing a way of looking at the world which permitted later generations to believe – mistakenly – that they were 'masters of nature', separate from, or above, natural processes. We are learning the hard way that this is simply not true. But instead of looking ahead at what this assumption implies for the future, our economic, political and educational systems remain caught up in the business of reproducing an obsolete past. And that is not all. Short-termism applies not just to business and investment; it penetrates our public and private lives too.

Evidence for the extent of the damage stemming from the Newtonian/Cartesian synthesis is extensive. It includes:

- the mass alienation of people from the planet's natural processes;

- the over-hyping of technology (especially the brave new world of information technology);
- thin and unlivable notions of what we mean by 'the present';
- the marginalisation of proposals concerning sustainable futures, and
- reductionisms like the emasculation of education into training, and equating data with both knowledge and wisdom.

In these conditions there is an enormous increase in anxiety and a growing sense that something important has gone wrong, that something essential has been subverted. None knows this better than the young.

OPTIMISM AND PESSIMISM AMONG YOUNG PEOPLE

Young people do not have to be persuaded to consider futures. Yet when they look ahead, they find many unsolved dilemmas which give them cause for serious concern. Survey after survey in many Western countries have shown that the young are fearful about the future, especially about issues like the production of nuclear weapons, environmental decline, and economic instability. These fears are reinforced by a deliberately confrontational, commercialised youth culture which extensively uses images of death, decay and destruction.

Too often the result is either that young people do not believe there will be a future or else they feel disempowered and helpless to act. Both responses undermine an individual's attempts to define his or her role in it. From there it is only a short step to all the substitute satisfactions and short-term instant gratifications that are offered within cultures obsessed with marketing and materialism.

We do not want to suggest that all young people feel helpless or depressed; many do not. However, the important thing about young people's fears and concerns is not their degree of optimism and pessimism, but the nature of the human responses which result from them. Some young people are naively optimistic, believing that 'everything will work out'. This kind of optimism is as dangerous as chronic pessimism, and both may lead to unproductive strategies of avoidance.

In a later chapter we suggest specific ways of helping young people to develop high-quality responses to their hopes and fears about the future. Let us simply note here that, given appropriate understanding and guidance, no young people need to remain depressed or fearful about their present or their future. While this may seem an exaggerated claim, it is entirely possible to consider every imaginable disaster which could occur, and still maintain an active and constructive attitude. Such shifts – from despair to empowerment – are critical for the future of civilisation. They depend most centrally upon the recovery of meaning.

THE RECOVERY OF MEANING

A major concern of this book is to indicate the grounds for the recovery of meaning within a reconstructed world-view. This is why chapter 4 considers a new 'map' about knowledge. Such an approach can help to re-establish some of the distinctions which have been overlooked or even discarded during the last two hundred years. A further step will be to look at other complementary understandings which extend this mapping process. Thus the sense of fragmentation, breakdown and loss of meaning which pervades post-modern cultures can be resolved in ways which are educationally sound and humanly productive. Human beings are not just passive recipients of pre-digested facts and meanings. We actively construct the world through our categories and ways of knowing. By carefully choosing which metaphors, assumptions and ways of knowing to adopt, we can build a more adequate frame of reference for many purposes, including education, an issue we return to in chapter 5.

It follows, then, that schools are in difficulty now not simply because of immediate, pragmatic issues, important as these may appear to be. Rather it is because within the present context – a context of compulsive technological dynamism, competitive individualism and a radical loss of meaning and purpose – schools are put in an impossible position. They stand at the crucial interface between past and future, charged both with the conservation of culture and with its radical renewal. Yet the rule book keeps changing; some pages are missing, others are unreadable, and some key terms like 'health', 'defence', 'progress', 'work' and 'leisure' no longer mean what they used to mean. No one could doubt that these are demanding times. As Schon (1971: 51) once put it:

a social system does not move smoothly from one state of its culture to another. . . . Something old must come apart in order for something new to come together. But for individuals within the system, there is no clear grasp of the next stable state – only a clear picture of the one to be lost. Hence, the coming apart carries uncertainty and anguish for the members of the system since it puts at risk the basis for self-identity that the system had provided.

Could there be a clearer explanation for the stress experienced by teachers and students? As the overlapping waves of social, technical, political, economic, cultural and environmental change have washed over us, so the structures, the continuities, expectations, values and meanings which once sustained the cultural landscape have weakened or dissolved entirely. Far from there being a coherent and integrated rationale to guide education, there is instead something of a human and cultural vacuum.

One consequence is that we flee to simplicities, like the regression from education to economics which is discussed below; another is the retreat from a difficult present to a safely reconstructed past. In such conditions it is very tempting to rebuild the museum cultures of yesteryear, to re-animate the great artists, writers, composers, explorers and pioneers, the philosophers, saints and sages of earlier times. It is obvious that these are of enduring value, but a return to the past is not enough on its own. Like the path to futures through spurious fantasies, the return to the past can be basically escapist. If we could somehow assemble the best of past and present but were still not interested in looking ahead, post-modern cultures and their school systems would still be in trouble.

If schools are to play a more culturally constructive role than they are doing at present, their work requires some broadly defined social purpose, something that goes beyond purely personal, economic and short-term considerations which derive solely from what has gone before. Though it may be unfashionable to say so, we badly need some sort of consensus which can sustain us through the years ahead. In short, educators need a credible vision of a future that works and that reconnects each individual with the wider world. They need a sustainable, human vision which embodies a set of viable purposes and meanings. How can such a vision be created?

THE SHIFT FROM PAST TO FUTURE TENSE

While there will always be differences of culture, value, viewpoint and interpretation among the human race, there remains a real prospect for a deep consensus about our social and cultural futures, and if this is the case there is a substantial basis for informed optimism. In the meantime, the single most effective change which schools can make is to operate as though they are already in the futures business.

Every act of planning, of deriving aims and objectives, of teaching and learning takes place not simply as the result of the push from the past but also because of the pull of the future. The powerful motivation supplied by ends and purposes forces us to look forward in time. As schools take up and use the available tools, methods and materials which have been developed over several decades, they will discover many new possibilities. Not least among them are ways of dealing with fear and depression about futures, ways of moving beyond the impasse toward futures which are both enterprising and creative.

One of the outcomes most often reported from well-grounded futures work in education is an increase in optimism and empowerment on the part of the students. This change in attitude arises in part because futures approaches help individuals to put things together, to create a workable synthesis from materials not usually available from within the confines of the standard academic culture. (This attitude change, incidentally, is true for teachers as well as for pupils.) A sense of qualified optimism also develops when students see that they are not helpless, and that they *can* make a difference. To develop a working familiarity with futures concepts and methods opens up new possibilities for understanding, for choice and for action at many levels. Instead of the future being abstract, a kind of empty space, it becomes instead a dynamic field of potentials which affects life in the present very profoundly indeed. Chapter 6 considers this shift in perspective more closely. Meanwhile, it is clear that educational systems are profoundly inhibited because of their close association with the industrial way of life and its curious manner of viewing the world; the problem is that our patterns of schooling have been built on basic assumptions which are now obsolescent.

THE GOOD NEWS

However, the good news is that we are at the beginning, not at the end, of the new story. There is plenty of good news to balance the bad, but it is often overlooked, marginalised, or not reported.

Educators not only understand the need to change but have usually been willing participants in the process. They know that education is absolutely pivotal to each country in the twenty-first century, and that a major rethinking is necessary. They will not willingly subscribe to an ideology for education which is inade-quate, unidimensional, and limiting for students. Furthermore, educators are well prepared to deliver major changes and have experience to call upon. They know that changes which emerge from economic rationalism and from the now defunct industrial world-view are literally a recipe for disaster.

What has emerged, then, is the need for a change of frame, a better way of envisioning schooling. The process of reconstruction begins with a willingness to identify and name those aspects of the dominant world-view which have clearly become redundant, and it continues with re-establishing purpose and meaning using a different set of assumptions, values and criteria. We try to help in this task with our analysis in the next three chapters. Thereafter, the key shift – the one which will affect all that follows – is to move the basis for action and planning from a now-completed past and towards an emergent, yet-to-be-created future. This is not primarily a technical process; rather it implies a deep-seated shift of meaning and purpose. Many people, and especially teachers and young people, have already demonstrated enormous creative and interpretive power in these areas. It is not as though we are in unknown territory. Let us give an example.

'If you want to change the world, then tell the kids first,' a teacher once said to us. He did not mean that the children need to be warned about the implications of what we intend to do, although that is important. Rather, he believed that children can help to bring about change in the wider community. Generating new ideas about the world and propagating them are tasks which can be entrusted to the young. If educators are persistent, systematic and consistent the process can be achieved largely through schools.

The point can be illustrated with an Australian example. During the 1970s, both the Cowell and the Cleve Area schools in South Australia's West Coast region developed fauna parks alongside their school premises containing animals indigenous to the district. The schools were helped by The Rev. Dr John Wittwer, the Lutheran pastor in the area who happened also to be a world authority on marsupials. The students acquired a genuine, well-informed, hard-nosed and caring attitude towards native animals, and it soon became evident that the children were causing a gentle transformation of community attitudes in those agricultural districts. One farmer would leave a stand of native trees instead of clearing it for cultivation. Another would replant an area with natural vegetation. Another would fence off a section of bushland known to be the habitat of a rare species of wallaby. Obviously, across the breakfast table and in many incidental ways, the youngsters were teaching their parents about conservation and about how to be sensitive custodians of the land and the delicate creatures which lived off it. No one is more effective at educating parents than children. So one way to transform prevailing world-views is to help young people teach adults!

The new framework, which we try to make explicit in the concluding chapters, is already being developed and is providing a better context for education. There appears to be an emerging consensus about several aspects of this new world-view:

• Firstly, the critique of the industrialised culture will change the way we conceive of society, work, wealth, living patterns and the nation-state. We deal with this aspect in chapter 2.
• Secondly, the condition of the planet and of its delicately balanced ecology is forcing people everywhere to think globally and to re-image their place in the world. This dimension is addressed in chapter 3.
• And thirdly, we have now gone well beyond scientific materialism and confidence in the scientific method as the one best way to knowledge, and have moved to a deliberate integration of the empirical, rational and spiritual dimensions in a more balanced 'map' of knowledge. This topic is treated in chapter 4.

By drawing upon such insights and sources, it is entirely possible to develop an informed optimism about human and cultural change, and to chart a more humanly compelling path into the twenty-first century. Indeed, do we have any other option? This book attempts to make the journey along that course less problematical and to set out for teachers and those associated with schools some of the major implications for education.

Chapter 2

Industrialism and its consequences

The earlier system of production, whether in agriculture or handicraft, developed in response to human needs and was dependent upon the energy derived mainly from plant growth, supplemented by animal, wind and water power . . . . This new industrial complex is based upon a group of postulates so self-evident to those who have produced the system that they are rarely criticised or challenged – indeed almost never examined – for they are completely identified with the new 'way of life.' . . .

First: man has only one all-important mission in life; to conquer nature. . . . To conquer nature is in effect to remove all natural barriers and human norms and to substitute artificial, fabricated equivalents for natural processes: to replace the immense variety of resources offered by nature by more uniform, constantly available products spewed forth by the machine.

From these general postulates a series of subsidiary ones are derived: there is only one efficient speed, *faster*; only one attractive destination, *farther away*; only one desirable size, *bigger*; only one rational quantitative goal, *more*. On these assumptions the object of human life, and therefore of the whole productive mechanism, is to remove limits, to hasten the pace of change, to smooth out seasonal rhythms and reduce regional contrasts – in fine, to promote mechanical novelty and destroy organic continuity.

Lewis Mumford, *The Pentagon of Power*, 1971

The most serious problems of modern society arise from the *success* of the industrial society paradigm. The horrors of modern warfare, worldwide environmental spoilation, interference with life-supporting ecological systems, progressive resource depletion, widespread poverty and hunger, prevalence of hazardous substances, stress-related disease, the possibility of detrimental climate change . . . all are interconnected components of what we might call the one world macroproblem. They are consequences of a mind-set and the behaviours and institutions associated with it . . . which brought great benefits in the past but now creates problems faster than it solves them. The world macroproblem will be satisfactorily resolved only through fundamental change of that mind-set.

Willis Harman, *Global Mind Change*, 1988

In this and the next two chapters, we discuss three macrochanges which have been taking a foothold across the world in the past few years, three perceptions about the way the world is, which, if accepted and acted on simultaneously, will effectively remake the meaning of our lives. We take each of them in turn and try to make clear the new attitudes and outlooks they produce. Nothing that we say should be new, for every reader will have come in contact with these changes in one form or another. We attempt here both to simplify and to synthesise, to make the ideas accessible, more easily understood, able to be seen in focus and then to be used.

TRANSITION TO A NEW KIND OF SOCIETY

The first of the three major factors is the transition from the industrial to the post-industrial state. It is a development which has taken place within the economic paradigm itself. Western societies during the twentieth century took as facts of life industrialisation, economic development, the production of goods to be bought and sold, and profit-making. But the ways of doing business have evolved so dramatically over the past two decades that the new patterns are radically changing international relationships, no less than our own lives. What those changes are and why they have come about need to be understood by the students now in school, and also by their parents and teachers. As well, the economic changes which underlie the new conditions rest on unexamined assumptions which are now being questioned, and appropriately so.

The onset of the Industrial Revolution in Europe coincided with the rise of modern science, especially the so-called Age of Enlightenment. Such a coincidence is not surprising, for the technologies on which the industrial economy depends were themselves made possible by the application of modern scientific methods. The Industrial Revolution which has had such a profound effect on European and North American societies over the past two hundred years was built on a number of related innovations. Central to each was the development of precision engineering and interchangeable parts. Specific technologies include the invention of the steam engine (which gave rise to cheap transportation, particularly through railroads and steam driven ships), electric power (upon which factories and cities rely for their survival), mechanisation (which transformed industries like mining), new materials (like steel and later plastics), and the internal combustion engine (which made the motor car and aeroplanes possible).

The pre-industrial society and the largely rural economy were profoundly changed by that transformation to an industrial society, for it brought in its train patterns like large-scale urbanisation, the growth of super-cities, the rise of a *nouveau riche* and a middle class, and the demands of factory production imposed on society, like the '9 to 5' working day.

The term the post-industrial state is not particularly satisfactory (because it is unidimensional), but it was coined to convey the idea that the developed world has now moved well beyond the kind of society in which factory production imposes a living style on most of the population. Indeed, it suggests that society is now undergoing another, major transformation in its history similar in impact to that of the onset of the Renaissance, the Reformation, or the Industrial Revolution. It is a 'qualitative and irreversible change', to quote Hirshchorn (1979: 288), as radically different as the shift in thinking and acting which occurred after Copernicus put forward the proposition that the sun and not the earth was at the centre of the universe.

THE NATURE OF THE TRANSFORMATION

In simple terms the post-industrial state is one in which manufacturing industry and large-scale factory production are not the prime employers of a country's workforce. How and where you earn your income influences your living patterns. For example, it affects where you buy your home, especially whether it is in a town, city, or the country; it determines what you can buy, and your life style; it usually helps to determine marriage patterns (because the partners often meet in a job-related setting), where the children of that marriage are educated, what the family's social contacts are, and so on. The nature of society, in short, is profoundly affected by how people make a living, and by what proportion of the workforce is employed in the different sectors of the economy.

In the post-industrial society, then, the industrial and manufacturing sectors of the economy lose their dominance over our lives in much the same way as the sector employing shepherds, farmers, and gardeners, the sector including village crafts, lost its dominance with the onset of the industrial society. Of course, manufacturing continues to operate in the post-industrial economy, as do rural industries, but they employ a comparatively smaller proportion of the workforce. As Daniel Bell, one of the first to write about the post-industrial state, put it,

A post-industrial society does not displace an industrial society, as the industrial society did not displace the agrarian society. Clearly the production of goods will be a feature of our society so long as we seek a rising standard of living. Yet these goods will be produced by fewer and fewer persons.

(Bell, 1976: 578)

What becomes clear, then, is that a displacement is occurring in many Western societies, and across several dimensions – economic, social, occupational, cultural. In consequence, there are some far-reaching accommodations which everyone must make, chiefly because many people will not be able to find jobs in the kinds of industries, firms, or occupations which may have employed them in the past, even the recent past.

Across the economically developed countries there has been a well-documented shift both in the way individual countries earn their wealth, and also in the way the people are employed. Until the late 1700s, for example, more than half the British labour force was employed in rural or agricultural industry. By the early 1980s, two centuries later, less than 3 per cent of the workforce was employed in that sector – a fall from one in two down to one in thirty of the workforce. At the turn of the twentieth century when industrialisation was in full swing, manufacturing accounted for over 40 per cent of employment in the so-called developed countries; it was close to 50 per cent in the period during and following the Second World War. The proportion is now in heavy decline. In France, West Germany and the United States, it had fallen to 22,

32 and 16 per cent respectively by 1986. Barry Jones (1982: 62) comments:

> Most sophisticated economies have, since the 1950s, been marked by an enormous growth in the output of manufacturing industry, accompanied by a steady fall in employment in that sector.

And that is the point. Higher profits are being made in manufacturing industry by using comparatively fewer people, by automation which replaces skilled labour, and by high technology.

If they are to find employment, people who might once have worked in agriculture, mining, and manufacturing will have to look elsewhere to find a job. In the post-industrial economy, generally speaking, employment expands in the services and information sectors, in those sectors which demand high-level training, such as in management, or in technology ('high tech'), or in human services like health and education. To demonstrate the point, the management consulting firm McKinseys estimated that by the year 2000, 5 per cent of the European community would produce all the agricultural products needed by Europe, 20 per cent would be involved in manufacturing industries, 25 per cent would be in manual services, and 50 per cent would be involved in some form of 'brain work' (quoted by Hayes and Watts, 1986: 16).

It was clear by the early 1980s that this new configuration for employment was going to cause problems. For example, Henderson, who led the poverty inquiry in Australia, drew attention to the fact that the service sectors were under heavy demand in some parts of the Australian economy, and were in urgent need of trained workers:

> From 1972–81, jobs in the tertiary or service sector increased by 850,000; in manufacturing they *fell* by 100,000. In community services alone employment increased by 366,000 from 1966–76.
> (Henderson, 1983: 32; italics ours)

The problem is that the economy was geared to the types of wealth creation characteristic of the industrial society which was in the process of being displaced, and there did not yet exist a way to fund the new burgeoning sectors. Thus, Henderson stated,

> education departments must reduce their high drop-out rates, and this requires [comparatively] more teachers. Many sections

of the health services need to expand; there are hospitals with wards closed because they cannot afford to pay nurses, mobile dental equipment to treat old people at home stands idle for lack of running expenses, and community health centres have lists of needs they would like to meet.

(ibid.)

Expanding employment in these services areas has a multiplier effect, he points out, because the newly employed 'spend and generate income for others'. But the fact remains that the new, service-based economy has to find a way of paying for these services. When permanent and simple jobs go out of existence through mechanisation, there is enormous pressure to provide community services, yet it is beyond the capacity of government (as presently constituted) to pay for them.

Using Australian statistics to demonstrate his point, Barry Jones demonstrates that in the post-industrial state employment grows in what he calls the tertiary, quaternary, and quinary sectors. The tertiary sector includes the 'tangible economic services, [like] transport, storage, retailing, utilities, repair and maintenance, police and armed services, and many personal services' (Jones, 1982: 65); this sector absorbed about a third of the Australian workforce. The quaternary sector is the information industry. By 1986, he points out (ibid.: 66–7), it had become the largest employer in Australia, accounting for about 38.7 per cent of all employment. More recently a report from the Australian House of Representatives Standing Committee on Long-Term Strategies put the figure at 41.5 per cent in 1981 (*Australia As An Information Society*, 1991). The figure is now certainly much higher. The quinary area involves 'domestic and quasi-domestic servicing' like catering, cleaning, some handcraft industries, and the businesses providing food, drink, and living quarters. Young people in particular need to be aware of how these employment configurations are changing, and what the implications are for them personally.

SO WHAT IN PARTICULAR CHANGES?

But changes in employment patterns have important ripple effects throughout society. Note how profoundly and in how many ways that earlier transition from the pre-industrial to the industrial state affected almost the entire range of social patterns. The transition to the post-industrial state will be at least as fundamental. While it is impossible to give a complete list, consider the following examples.

- The transition to industrialisation saw the eclipse of cottage industries (which were village-based), the decline of the centrality of rural industries (people in fact left the land and migrated to cities), and the supplanting of both by the large factory.
- To ensure that those new, manufacturing industries could be run, thousands of factory and process workers were needed. So there grew up around the factories huge urban conglomerations – the modern city, in fact. The workers abandoned rural areas and clustered in densely populated dormitory suburbs and towns.
- The style and tempo of life, once geared to the village and the land, now became metropolitan. Most important in terms of social interactions, where one worked and where one lived became physically separated. The time sense speeded up, became dissociated from seasonal rhythms and became linear. For a while at least, a new sense of the future came into focus.
- New people joined the ruling class, and many dropped out of it. The new merchants became rich; and the middle class – as we have come to know it over the past two centuries – came into existence, with common characteristics like upward mobility, a search for promotion, and the 'Protestant work ethic'. Thus the new wealth was gained not from inheritance or from being born into property (as was the case in the feudal, pre-industrial society), but largely from being a manufacturer, from putting on to a factory production line those operations which were once performed by hand.
- The pre-industrial economy tended to depend upon extractive industries like hunting, fishing, farming and mining; we still call these 'primary industries'. The industrial economy, on the other hand, is based upon manufacturing, on the production and selling of goods; we call this sector 'secondary industry'. The post-industrial economy encourages services to business and to people (the services we tend to label 'professional'); and also firms providing and processing information – indeed we call it 'know-how', data-processing, information technology.
- The work done in the pre-industrial era was dependent on

nature, on the seasons and the weather. The working day was governed by sunrise and sunset, by whether it was wet or dry, by the seasonal rotation of sowing and harvest. The industrial revolution, on the other hand, invented machine time, the clock. Since factories operate under a roof, the working day and the working year became standardized, almost independent of the seasons. It also produced a rush-hour when workers went to and from work, their arrival, departure and lunch break being regulated by the machines of production. In the post-industrial state, the 9-to-5 day does not make much sense because many fewer people have their working time tied to the factory day. Time then becomes relative, day and night may merge or be used differentially, and many will operate on international time, as is the case with financial services, the tourism and entertainment industries, and with the sports industries. The seasons have almost no effect, since people can commute to other parts of the planet to find such things as a holiday climate.

- In the pre-industrial society, where village crafts and rural industries were the chief sources of income, success depended upon muscle power and manual skills. In the industrial society, technical skill became prized, for economic success depended on electrical power and energy, on machines and on the skill of the people who service them. In the post-industrial state, success depends heavily on brain power, on what one knows (know-how), on what knowledge one has access to, on the flows of information, on professional and technological skill. Thus there is a huge difference in the educational levels in the three states.

- In consequence, whereas the pre-industrial society relied on skilled craftsmen and artisans, or on farming skills, and the industrial economy depends on technicians and tradespersons (it needs a large number of them), the post-industrial economy rewards the well educated specialist, the professional, the one with expertise, information, and managerial skills.

- As a result of these workplace changes, there are enormous transformations in how people relate to each other. In the pre-industrial society, people lived largely in small communities, usually rural towns and villages. They formed closely knit, insular communities; there were interactions at many levels but among a relatively small number of persons. Urbanisation is a major characteristic of the industrial society; most of the people tend to live in large cities or in a megalopolis. Indeed, the newly industrialised countries (the so-called NICs) of the late-twentieth century face enormous problems because of the growth of super-cities, the unplanned urban sprawl which accompanies the rapid transition to industrialisation and citification. On the other hand, a post-industrial society can literally dispense with the city. People tend to operate in the 'global village', and are connected to an international network or community in which one identifies with people in another suburb, province or country almost as easily as with the strangers who live in one's own street.

- And, of course, commerce is different in each of the states. The pre-industrial society tended to be relatively local, although barter gave way to local markets, to small and regionally focused businesses. In the industrial economy, large companies and large government emerged. It was the period of national economies, of government regulation, of national corporations; the distinctions between small and large business became significant. Interestingly, the word 'marketplace' is still used in the industrial economy, but it has a very different meaning now from the place where the village market was conducted. In the post-industrial state, the multinationals, the corporate giants, and the conglomerate firms operate across national boundaries, creating an interlocking, interdependent world economy. In the process, governments tend to lose much of the power to control their own economies.

THE ECONOMIC IMPERATIVE

It should not surprise us, then, that as the post-industrial conditions began to take effect, economics seemed to pervade and transform everything. The decade of the 1980s saw an economic framework used as the rationale for almost every major policy initiative, certainly public policies, a change so complete that it was almost heresy to oppose or to question it. Presumably the need for any country to reshape its economy so that it could compete in the international marketplace, especially alongside aggressive performers like West Germany, Japan, South Korea, Taiwan, Singapore and India, has become so overwhelming that it makes the subordination of all other enterprises to that single economic cause almost a matter of national loyalty.

Thus there developed across the world an interlocking economic order which began to surmount national economies, making them dependent on each other. The movements on the New York and Tokyo stock exchanges, for example, cause fluctuations in the value of local currencies which cannot be controlled by governments. Australian mineral production ebbs and flows with the needs of Japanese industry. Farm subsidies in Europe directly affect the markets served by Australian and New Zealand primary industries. International markets, not local needs, determine the extent of logging activity in the Philippines. Fluctuating exchange rates do wild things to the level of any country's foreign indebtedness. Even financial enterprises like banks become flotsam on that economic sea. In a real sense, then, the end of the twentieth century saw national governments at the mercy of the international marketplace.

It was the Western economies – for so long the engines of world trade – which felt the impact of the new international economic conditions most severely. Industrialisation in particular had given them their comparative wealth, but by the last decade of the century they found themselves competing against the newly industrialised countries (NICs) where cheaper labour is available and which can buy the most recently developed technology to outpace old 'smoke stack industries'. Indeed, manufacturing industry and large-scale factory production themselves underwent fundamental transformations, shedding labour because of increased automation.

As we would expect from transformations of this kind within societies and around the world, the proportion of the workforce in the various occupations changed radically by the 1990s. Declining employment and rising efficiencies in rural production, particularly wheat, caused an international trade war and charges of dumping. Employment in manufacturing fell proportionately; whereas in the 1950s over 40 per cent of workers in the industrial West earned their living in manufacturing industry, by the 1980s it had fallen to about 20 per cent (Jones, 1982: 62; Hayes and Watts, 1986: 16; Bell, 1976: 578; Henderson, 1983: 32). And employment burgeoned in the information and the services industries (Jones 1982: 65–7), where it was predicted four jobs in every five would soon be located.

EDUCATION AND THE NEW ECONOMIC CONDITIONS

But here is the rub; there are some profound, indeed funda-mental, ways in which education and training must be transformed in the post-industrial society. These are transformations which teachers, students and their parents need to understand, for the changes will affect them deeply.

The first feature to note is that education, whether for good or ill, becomes integrated with the economy, for those new growth areas in the economy tend to be heavily dependent on education and training. They are the sectors where a majority of professions and 'emerging professions' are practised, and they make use of a plethora of specialisations. A country has little chance of developing a sound post-industrial economy based on these areas unless it has the backing of a well educated community which values those specialist skills (and will pay for them) or unless there exists within the country the depth and range of training programmes which will keep up a supply of the skilled people necessary to make these areas competitive. It is in these sectors that the most rapid developments occur in a post-industrial economy.

These sectors are characterised by the kind of specialisations which must be acquired through tertiary education. They assume that each worker has completed twelve years of secondary edu-cation, for upon that foundation are built vocational skills, learned in vocational training programmes after leaving school. Further-more, it is substantial and formal training of the kind which leads to a paper qualification and which forms the passport to practise in these occupations. Usually such a passport is needed no matter where in the world the person chooses to practise. Educational qualifications, in short, have become an international currency.

It is hardly surprising, then, that in country after country, just at the time when each was attempting the fundamental transition out of an industrially dependent economy into a post-industrial one, schools in particular came under such intense pressure and were subject to such adverse criticism. Put simply, education is the pivotal factor on which depends that shift in the economy. On the education sector devolves the question of whether a country can quickly upgrade the general capacity of its entire workforce to enable its people to be easily deployed in those occupations which ensure success in the new international economic conditions. Further, that education must be internationally viable.

By the 1990s, therefore, secondary education in particular was beginning to operate with an international perspective. It is no longer sufficient for schools to be parochial or insular about their curricula or about the performance levels of their students, for those students, on leaving school, are finding themselves increasingly in an international workplace where they function alongside or compete with people from neighbouring countries. What is learnt at school by young people of their own age in Japan, Canada, South America, South Korea, India, Russia or Thailand is relevant to them. It is no longer good enough for students to compare themselves and their school records only with their peer group in their own school, in their own province or State, or in their own country.

Thus *education is itself an integral part of the burgeoning sectors of a post-industrial economy*. Indeed it is one of the most significant parts of both the information and the services sectors. With nursing and social welfare, education makes up the largest part of the human services sector. It is hardly surprising, then, that education is so widely spoken of in business terms, or that it is referred to as an export industry. People acknowledge that education is itself an information industry by their very willingness to buy and sell their knowledge. Nor should it surprise us that the favoured mode for delivering the service is a privatised one, and that the public or government-provided schools are constantly being told to emulate the style of operation which has characterised the private, stand-alone schools.

In short, the quality of schooling has become one of the fundamental factors determining whether a country's entire workforce can acquire the competencies to support the industries on which a post-industrial economy relies. In addition, the whole community must be sufficiently educated not only to value the new kinds of skill and knowledge but also to reward with suitable salaries those who have them.

The most obvious consequence of the post-industrial conditions is that preconceived notions about education, employment, careers, and the workplace will have to change. In particular, post-industrial societies tend to rebuild their occupational training programmes, most of which are now likely to require twelve years of schooling as their entry level; they will be, in other words, post-school programmes. In such a society, at least a year's post-school training comes to be seen as necessary for everyone.

At the same time, multiple channels develop to allow those who are displaced from the workforce to be retrained for another job. Education is always a better alternative than unemployment; and paying a training wage is a better investment for both the government and industry than paying unemployment benefits or a redundancy package.

In terms of skill development, post-industrial conditions bring a movement away from a high degree of specialisation which leaves the worker vulnerable to job changes. The favoured option is multi-skilling, whereby the worker becomes capable of operating in several domains. Training tends to focus on 'generic skills' which are basic to a number of areas. At least initially, the worker will be more of a generalist than was the case a decade earlier, and the job-specific skills will be taught within the industry itself, or in cooperation between a firm and a technical institute. New hybrids in occupational skills also grow up in this kind of economy. The Japanese, for example, developed mecatronics, a combination of mechanical and electronics training; and new combinations or disciplines are formed like biotechnology (enginering and biology), genetic engineering, and so-called artificial intelligence.

FROM INDUSTRIAL TO POST-INDUSTRIAL CITIES

There is a further transformation about education in the post-industrial economy. Since universal schooling grew up in the industrial era and was patterned on factory production, for the most part schools tend to be conceived of as urban or suburban institutions. In industrialised countries, most of the small rural schools are progressively closed as the rural workforce declines. Larger schools (like larger businesses) bring economies of scale, and they provide parental choice (as though the parents are customers shopping around for the best bargains). Schooling becomes identified with cities and towns.

We know that the huge cities which have grown up around the globe during the past century are a direct result of the industrial revolution. Put simply, people had to congregate in suburbs around the industrial cities in order to supply the workforce to drive the mass production of factory-based industries. In the process, supercities are now racked with a host of personal, political, and environmental problems. The large and usually urbanised secondary school was not only created by industrialisation, but it has also played a decisive role in fostering the social patterns of the industrialised society.

The post-industrial economy therefore ought to allow us to be more intelligent about the way we plan and run the cities of the future, and in the same process it will provide other models (and locations) for schooling. We do not need to go on building, or allowing to develop, the kinds of cities which reproduce the multiple social diseases of the industrial economy. The hi-tech city is of course a brainchild of the post-industrial society, the new economy displacing the workforce out of factory production.

The industrial economy and the super-city also bred class consciousness. There were vast enclaves of working class people clustered around the engines of industrial growth – factory production, steel, shipping, motor vehicle construction. So the industrial city tended to stratify society along lines of social class. Liverpool; Manchester; Birmingham; the ports of London or New York or Singapore or Shanghai or Hong Kong; Rotterdam; Pittsburgh; Detroit; Chicago – all across the world, we are now witnessing the consequences of the boom-and-bust of these industrial cities, and they have characteristics in common.

- A large, industrial area – ugly, run-down, with hectares of land occupied by factories, industrial barns and warehouses; or partially derelict docklands now laid waste by computerised bulk-handling and containerized cargo facilities. (As these areas are redeveloped, where will 'the school' belong?)
- A central business district (CBD), built on the assumption that it is necessary (it no longer is, of course) for commercial and business houses and the headquarters of major firms to be physically and geographically close to each other. They were usually devoid of schools.
- A run-down inner rim of suburbs, once the homes of the well-to-do, but now vacated by the rich who have moved to the semi-garden, outer rim of suburbs, close to parklands and green belts. The inner suburbs became slums, with run-down residences owned by absentee landlords and over-occupied by poorer families who live in constricted space in order to meet the rents. The schools in these areas acquire a reputation of being 'disadvantaged' or 'working-class'.

- These suburbs are then regenerated by the yuppies, the younger two-income, no-family, professional couples, who need a commuting pad close to the central business district and the down-town facilities like theatre and restaurants. They do not need a local school, and will not support it.
- Large areas of suburbs divided along lines of social class, with schools divided along the same lines.

If there is one lesson the world can learn from the industrial revolution, it is surely that we can plan cities more cleverly than this. It is the large industrial cities, with all their consequences, which constitute the planet's major source of pollution and the environment's grossest enemy. We now realise that they cannot be allowed to go on mindlessly multiplying, at least, not in that form. Importantly, education, and particularly schools, ought not to replicate those same patterns.

NEW MANAGERIALISM; ORGANISATIONS CHANGE TOO!

The cities took the shape they did in part because of the kind of large-scale organisation thought appropriate for success in the industrial economy. Bureaucracy therefore became the almost universal form of organisation; in fact, it was described by Weber as an 'ideal form'. It was predictable, its purpose and operations were rational, its routines were systematic and rarely changed, and it was large-scale, capable of making routine the activities of literally thousands of people. It was an organisational structure built on the analogy to a machine.

A post-industrial society changes all that, and it produces organisations quite different from what they were in the past. For example, there are new rules for work or employment. A fee for service tends to replace a salary or fixed income; one is rewarded for performing a task rather than for turning up at nine o'clock. There is a known and direct link between effort or skill and productivity or profit. In the new economic order, it becomes clear that the world does not owe us a living.

Many post-industrial firms are therefore small, or else they are configured to accommodate relatively self-contained minifirms operating inside the larger firm. Describing the post-industrial firm in 1986, Hayes and Watts (1986: 34) comment that

work will be undertaken in small, semi-autonomous, task-oriented units linked by computers to a central base. These small units, like atoms, will. . . [be] bonded like molecules into a strong corporate entity via carefully nurtured cultural bonds.

Deal and Kennedy call this format an 'atomised organisation'. Increasingly, too, the workers are regarded as stakeholders in the company; often they will partly own the company they work in, and they will be sophisticated about enterprise, the private sector, management and finance. They work in an international setting.

FACTORY IMAGERY ABOUT SCHOOLS

It is chastening to realise how heavily school organisation draws upon the factory model of organisation. Teachers often refer to the head as 'the boss'; teacher unions encourage a 'workers versus management' mentality, and engage in 'industrial action'. Schools abound with the characteristics of bureaucracy, like hierarchy and positional status; they encourage upward mobility and promotion through graded ranks; they teem with rules and regulations, with specialists and divisions of functions. Terms like 'at the chalk face' suggest that education can be likened to a mining and processing industry. Again there are parallels in both teacher-talk and educational practices for business choice, competition, a buyer's market, privatisation, encouraging small enterprises, decentralisation, diversification and product excellence.

Since mass schooling, including compulsory elementary and secondary education, was a direct outcome of the industrial system, we would expect such a range of industrial metaphors to be used. Factory imagery, part and parcel of the industrial paradigm, is almost endemic to the model of schooling as we presently know it. Terms like 'learning outcomes', 'outputs', 'processes', the 'end-product of schooling' and the 'products of the system' are all metaphors derived from a factory producing goods and products. Academic 'progress' conjures up imagery about conveyor belts and assembly lines, about learning components and curriculum modules, production units and specialist parts. It is no wonder that people so readily accept the language about 'standards', 'grades' and 'credentials' as though these are trademarks stamped on 'the finished product', the students who have been 'processed' in a standard way.

In fact, the big school was designed and organised like a factory.

Much of the terminology still used in schools is based upon metaphors derived both from factories and from the medieval society, especially feudal armies and the centralised church hierarchies (Beare, 1987). The idea of compulsory schooling has grown out of and been based on ideas drawn from the industrialised society. We should therefore *not* expect the secondary school to survive in its present form into the post-industrial society.

But the current shift of describing education in largely economic terms carries other dangers for everyone. To those operating from the viewpoint of economic rationality, this shift is a seductive one; it simplifies educational governance, it legitimises 'efficiency' and ties what looks like an amorphous and labrynthine institution firmly to defined goals and purposes. From there it is a short step to seeing 'efficiency, effectiveness, equity and (market) excellence' as the four Es of education. The concern has now gone far beyond questions of economic controls or financial accountability. It has become a paradigmatic one, for the public conception of education has been redefined into an economic framework, which uses a new vocabulary about schooling based upon the idea of markets.

INSTRUMENTALISM AND THE ECONOMIC WORLD-VIEW

So there is no avoiding changes to schools. Every school system we have read about or visited in the last ten years has been confronted with the need to restructure in the face of the economic paradigm. For example, schools around the world appear to have the same agenda: to set priorities, to trim expenditures and to save scarce education dollars. To be good economic managers, those running education enterprises have borrowed the devices of business, commerce and financial departments (Harman *et al.*, 1991: 308–19; Beare, 1989b).

The signs are very clear and as always it is common language, especially its recurring metaphors, which give the clues. That part of the public education enterprise responsible for running schools now tends to be absorbed inside an even bigger firm called an Education Ministry, a kind of corporate takeover. The terms 'corporate management', 'corporate plan' and 'corporate structure' are literally used in the documentation about educational reorganisation. Such terminology and the rationale which goes with it are now widespread. Conventional thinking is like that; it not only throws up consistent ideas but it also produces predictable and stereotyped responses.

NATIONAL INTERVENTIONS, NATIONAL POLICIES.

The economic world-view also takes another powerful form, namely the assertion of national priorities, not least in education. National pressure is clearly linked with a standard view of economic growth. In this approach, the aim is to maximise each nation's competitive advantage in the international trading game. The rules of this game are seldom questioned, the assumption being that growth is good, and the more growth the more wealth.

Yet growth according to industrial definitions has not been a complete success. Indeed, the growth paradigm has become increasingly problematic as the costs have mounted. There is increasing evidence that the long-term necessity for economic activities to be sustainable makes old-style notions of growth and profits untenable. Indeed the meanings we attach to the notion of wealth have also shifted.

The assertion of national priorities for education is clearly an attempt to exert centralised control, to assert government objectives, and to formalise the link between education and economics. To use an Australian example, the then federal Minister for Education, Senator Susan Ryan, declared in 1986 that 'education and the world of work' were at 'the heart of our government's economic strategy . . . and our national objectives.' She went on to say that 'efficiency and equity are the key defining terms for this government's achievements', and that 'getting the education system right is essential for our plans', because it was 'the most efficient and the most equitable instrument which a national government has to push along change, reform and growth.' (Beare 1987: 74)

The intervention of governments and the economic imperatives have forced a semantic shift of profound, and perhaps sinister, significance. If education is continually described in economic terms, if it is continually made to conform to economic models and if the vocabulary of economics is repeatedly used, then there comes a time when education itself is understood primarily in terms of a business enterprise. When it is redefined as a business corporation, there will have occurred a paradigm shift with enormous consequences.

So while it is clear why education has been pushed into an economic frame of reference which not only defines its place in society but also rephrases the way it describes its purposes, the underpinnings of this great exercise in control are not as firm as is commonly believed. Governments tend to want to play the old industrial game better, whereas the game itself has changed.

TRANSCENDING THE INDUSTRIAL MODEL

Wherever this approach has been used, and it is ubiquitous in post-industrial economies, it has run up against an intractable problem, namely that some of the most highly valued outcomes of schooling can neither be measured nor even described in this way. The economic paradigm imposes a vocabulary and a mode of viewing the world which puts some of the best aspects of education outside the frame of reference.

How, for example, do you put a mathematical or economic weight on increasing a child's self-esteem, or on developing a love of reading, on enjoying good literature and music, on building racial tolerance, or on valuing qualities like loyalty, self-control and human affection? We have always known that the outcomes of education are difficult to quantify reliably, and that some of the most deeply valued things about life, no less than education, cannot be judged according to a purely economic calculus. The economic approach encourages instrumentalism, valuing things because they are immediately useful or directly measurable. It is exactly this process of reductionism which is so characteristic of the rationality of the industrial era; if something cannot be measured, it is either unimportant or imaginary.

In summary, then, the logic of the international economy, even though itself limited, has now replaced much of the thinking which was taken for granted during the two hundred years of the industrial state. The new understandings have tended to be couched in economic terms. But the economic frame of thinking is now seen as partial and seriously flawed in several important ways, and the very notion of industrialism is being overtaken by some of the considerations which we now turn to in chapters 3 and 4.

Before we do so, however, it must be clearly understood that social life, the world of work, the international community and education itself are all in the process of being transformed by the macroshift from an industrial to a post-industrial society. Even if the assumptions underlying the world economy are not questioned, there will still be a huge, fundamental, and intentional change, and schools are already being made to adapt to it. This one factor alone will force schools in the twenty-first century to operate in ways quite different from what has been accepted over recent decades. We discuss some of the aspects of such schooling in chapter 5.

Chapter 3

Global consciousness
The one-world view

Biodance – the endless exchange of the elements of living things with the earth itself – proceeds silently, giving us no hint that it is happening. It is a dervish dance, animated and purposeful and disciplined; and it is a dance in which every living thing participates.

These observations simply defy any definition of a static and fixed body. Even our genes, our claim to biologic individuality, constantly dissolve and are renewed. We are in a persistent equilibrium with the earth.

Yet the boundary of our body has to be extended even further than the earth itself. We know that certain elements in our body, such as the phosphorus in our bones, were formed at an earlier stage in the evolution of the galaxy. Like many elements in the earth's crust, it was cycled through the lifetime of several stars before appearing terrestrially, eventually finding its way into our body.

A strictly bounded body does not exist. The concept of a physical I that is fixed in space and that endures in time is at odds with our knowledge that living structures are richly connected with the world around them. Our roots go deep; we are anchored in the stars.

Larry Dossey, *Space, Time and Medicine*,1982

All our laws and constitutions and political philosophies are descended from parables about social interaction, framed by images of the environments in which human beings relate, shaped by information about how one person's actions impact upon another life. . . . The dimensions of the frame are considerably less than global. . . . Now, suddenly, the frame expands.

Walter Anderson, *To Govern Evolution*, 1987

In 1988 the United Nations published the Brundtland Report titled *Our Common Future*. It was the result of the deliberations of a panel of international experts chaired by the prime minister of Norway and convened as the World Commission on the Environment and Development. The report begins with the following paragraph, which is repeated at the end as a kind of reprise.

In the middle of the 20th century, we saw our planet from space for the first time. Historians may eventually find that this vision had a greater impact on thought than did the Copernican revolution of the 16th century . . . . From space, we see a small and fragile ball dominated not by human activity and edifices but by a pattern of clouds, oceans, greenery, and soils. Humanity's inability to fit its doings into that pattern is changing planetary systems, fundamentally. Many such changes are accompanied by life-threatening hazards. This new reality, from which there is no escape, must be recognised – and managed.

(Brundtland Report, 1988: 1, 308)

Earth, the report says, is 'an organism whose health depends on the health of all its parts', and that balance can now be achieved only by deliberate action on humanity's part. Some of the actions of individual human beings, of institutions and of nations can best be described as diseases within that body, the earth. Indeed, some of the consequences of human behaviour, like the greenhouse effect, can be likened to cancers; they may indeed be terminal illnesses for planet Earth unless we very quickly do something about them. The report speaks of the 'downward spiral' caused by the interlocking of economic systems with ecological ones, and warns that doing nothing about that spiral is no longer an acceptable option. In short, business-as-usual outlooks are no longer viable.

The report makes the important point that administering the cure will devolve largely upon those who are now young people. Most of today's decision-makers will be dead by the time Earth feels the full impact of illnesses like 'acid precipitation, global warming, ozone depletion, or widespread desertification and species loss. But most of the young voters today will still be alive'. The report points out that, as the Commission collected its evidence, 'it was the young, those with the most to lose, who were the harshest critics of the planet's present management' (ibid.: 8).

The report attempts to outline an achievable strategy to restore balance to the life of the planet. It says that although the Commissioners came from twenty-one different countries, they were able to agree about the plan. So 'the present generation must begin now, and begin together, nationally and internationally' to put it into effect. 'We are unanimous in our conviction that the security, well-being, and very survival of the planet depend on such changes, now' (ibid.: 343).

Governments around the world are beginning to adopt the report's approaches, and the term 'sustainable development' has found its way into the vernacular. The report therefore provides further evidence of the profound change in attitude which seems to be occurring in the way we perceive ourselves and the earth we inhabit.

In the first two chapters we showed that the world community has moved out of the Industrial Revolution frameworks, away from classical industrialism, and has begun to take on new patterns, even though the mind-set and consciousness of the older order still remain powerfully present. There is a new globalism developing throughout the world, which supersedes merely economic considerations. Since those working with the students now in school are already engaged with the people who will be living most of their lives within the new context, it is important for educators to attempt their own synthesis.

FROM FRAGMENTATION TO A NEW GLOBAL AWARENESS

In chapters 1 and 2 we referred to major intellectual shifts which seemed to be occurring across a range of disciplines, like medicine, education, the social sciences, economics, government, psychology, religion and politics; the shifts are consistent, and all of a piece. We emphasised that the frameworks which have propped up social and scientific conventions over the last two centuries rest on some questionable assumptions. To put it briefly, the Western/industrial world-view was based on certainty, predictability, control and rationality, all outgrowths of modern science and its necessary concomitant, scientific materialism. They concentrated on those narrow aspects of reality which can be subjected to empirical examination and measurement. Equally, however, scientific approaches tend to be sceptical about core values and beliefs, about magic and enchantment, about mythologies and religious experiences. Yet these domains have their own intrinsic qualities, not least of which is integration, the knitting together of diffuse pieces of knowledge into a wider and more coherent pattern.

Until very recently the scientific approach has been to fragment knowledge. It broke 'reality' down into component pieces which were then subjected to rigorous scrutiny. By understanding the multitude of parts, accounts could be constructed of the whole. But each of the parts became someone's territory, specialisations produced border disputes and territoriality, and knowledge areas became esoteric, only accessible to the experts in that particular discipline. Science has therefore had a tendency to fracture and compartmentalise our views.

However, when we stand back from our neatly developed specialised outlooks, it becomes apparent from both a global and a cosmic perspective that life on earth involves a web of interactions which are tangled with past, present and future; and that human beings are simply members of a species of five billion living entities which are literally making and unmaking the space they inhabit, to the point of threatening the planet's capacity to support life itself. The extent of the damage being caused by the dominant world-view is clearly frightening (Mumford, 1971; Berman, 1981) and is bound to breed pessimism about the future.

Those who live in cities form the greater part of humankind. Yet city dwellers are divorced from the myriad of species which live in the natural or unspoiled parts of the planet, especially wilderness areas. Industrialisation has insulated entire populations from the simpler patterns of life lived close to nature. In these conditions there is an enormous increase in anxiety about our existence, as though something essential to the world's well-being has been subverted. Indeed, Frankl suggests that an important part of the world's problem is a systematic frustration of the will to meaning, now usurped by a will to power or a will to pleasure (Frankl, 1959).

During the years of expansion following the Second World War, it suited those in power to support an ideology which drew its inspiration and rationale from the past, but in present conditions we require more credible models, coherent visions of a variety of futures in order to guide our choices about the present. There is a large gap between the speed and significance of change and our capacity to articulate, or even to imagine, credible future altern-atives. A recent survey of scenarios for Australia's future ended by stating that 'the literature search failed to uncover a single major scenario which argued for a positive, strongly optimistic view of Australia's future toward 2000' (Barr, 1988: 66). However, it is important to realise that it is not necessary to remain despairing and alienated by an inadequately understood present. It is entirely possible to renegotiate a future, or futures, worth living in (Slaughter, 1987a). Since the human brain/mind system can range at will through past, present and multiple futures, there is no necessary reason for us to to experience catastrophe before we take steps to counteract it.

CONCERNS ABOUT BIAS AND DISCONNECTEDNESS

In this context, our understanding of modern science has been affected by a new consciousness about the planet. Science is not value-free, we discover. It is not independent of bias, at arm's length from prejudice or from the distortions of orthodoxy. James Lovelock, the researcher who invented the Gaia hypothesis about the planetary system and who carries on his work outside of estab-lishment laboratories, comments that

> nearly all scientists are employed by some large organization, such as a governmental department, a university, or a multi-national company. Only rarely are they free to express their science as a personal view. They are constrained by official frameworks and attitudes, by the 'tribal rules of the discipline', by peer reviews, by conventional wisdom of one kind or another.

> (Lovelock, 1988: xiv)

In short, the patterns of extending knowledge and the scientific processes themselves are also to an extent culture-bound, circum-scribed, and compartmentalised. The old world-view can be very subtle in its operation, yet the effects are powerful.

The way human beings have organised themselves into com-munities is affected by the same fractured world-view. The nation-state in its monolithic form, however, is becoming obsolete, and many of the institutions and power structures which took shape in the industrial era may be reaching the end of their useful lives, in part because they tend to persist in enforcing and sustaining limited interests rather than universal ones. For example, the imperatives of merchandising promote the misleading strategy that people must function primarily *as consumers* in order to survive, and millions have believed it. The result is that little attention is paid to the fragility and interconnectedness of the world or to the limited nature of the earth's resources. Instead, it seems, many of the best minds are devoted to the abstracted nullities of money, profit and power, as lucidly described two decades ago by Lewis Mumford (Mumford 1971). This is a system which feeds upon itself, devours its own children and is parasitic upon the shared foundations of life. Yet, when properly understood, this otherwise depressing picture also offers a powerful stimulus to rise above the compulsive escapism of cultures in crisis.

It is too superficial, then, to argue that Western cultures are in a state of crisis merely because of commercial greed, because they are ungovernable, because of this or that technology, or because their patterns of social organisation are faulty. The crisis has more profound roots; it comes from inadequate ways of knowing and from an only partially comprehended understanding of connectedness. In the next chapter, therefore, we shall consider what are described as reductionistic epistemologies and the problems produced by what Wilber calls 'category errors' (Wilber, 1979).

For our purposes here, it should be recognised that the Western world-view is now being seen as fragmented, not connected; it tends to isolate consequences, rather than admitting how networked they are. If that kind of isolationist thinking is allowed to persist and to feed present trends, it will lead to a future few of us would wish to live in. But exactly at the point where the Newtonian paradigm ends, an entire new world of significance begins, not only because modern physics has changed our view of reality (Bohm, 1980), but also because so many people have had direct experience of other states of knowing and being, and have left us their accounts (Huxley, 1945). New possibilities for individuals and cultures exist precisely because clearer insights, creativity, and certain forms of spiritual practice have had the effect of refining the way we perceive and know the world. These are views which integrate, which encourage us to put things together again. As wisdom deepens and as we base our behaviours on it, so we may progressively transform the wider world of which we are the most highly developed part.

Precisely what sort of world-view is emerging? Many books are being written on this topic and it is beyond the scope of this one to be definitive. But the main themes which permeate the new structures of thinking and perception are fairly clear. These themes ought now to underlie all school programmes, and inform the basic assumptions on which school curricula are built.

THE 'ONE WORLD' PARADIGM

We suggested above that the so-called Newtonian/Cartesian synthesis constructed a way of looking at the world which allowed later generations to believe that they were masters of nature. We added that economic, political and educational systems are still caught up in the business of reproducing aspects of an obsolete world-view.

But there is now occurring internationally a shift in the way we image ourselves as cohabitors of this planet. Its political manifestation is visible, in part, through the green movement, or the conservation movement, worldwide. The idea whose time has come, and which will certainly pervade thinking through the next decade, is this: *the globe is itself a single, delicately balanced, living organism, and human beings are merely one species in that incredible ecosystem.* Capra (1982: 32) puts it like this:

> The universe is no longer seen as a machine, made up of a multitude of separate objects, but appears as a harmonious, indivisible whole, a network of dynamic relationships that include the human observer and his or her consciousness in an essential way.

In the same way, Laughlin and Richardson (1986: 411) comment that 'the lack of systems consciousness is . . . the single greatest danger to this planet'. Put positively, there is now a growing international awareness that the entire earth is a living system, and that human action affects and is connected with the planet's health.

In part at least, we owe the new perceptions to James Lovelock. In 1979, Lovelock startled the scientific establishment with his book called *Gaia: A New Look at Life on Earth* (1979). 'Existing theories held that plants and animals evolve on, but are distinct from, an inanimate planet', but Lovelock advanced the view – based upon quite impressive computer simulations, the so-called Daisyworld model – 'that the Earth, its rocks, oceans and atmosphere, and all living things are part of one great organism, evolving over the vast range of geological time' (Lovelock, 1988). His thesis, then, is that Earth itself is 'a coherent system of life, self-regulating, self-changing, a sort of immense organism' (Lovelock, 1988: x). His later book, titled *The Ages of Gaia: a Biography of Our Living Earth* (1988), again describes the history of the earth from that perspective.

Since the earth is alive, it can also become sick. Lovelock points out that those who practise medicine must subscribe to the Hipprocratic Oath, and accept the proposition that they will do everything to preserve the life of the patient. At the present time, Lovelock tells us, those whose work influences the health of planet Earth need to take a similar kind of oath, especially since some of the treatments to heal the earth have 'consequences more severe than those of the poison' (Lovelock, 1988: xviii). Other observers have pointed out that some North American Indian cultures routinely considered the possible effects of actions and decisions on future generations before they proceeded to implement them.

It is of considerable significance to recognise that most earlier and less technically sophisticated cultures understood these dangers. One of the clearest examples is the much-quoted letter of Chief Seattle to the president of the United States in 1855. The letter is often treated as an evocation of a pre-industrial sensibility, but it is more precisely both a description and a critique of the enormous negative impact of Western rapaciousness upon the natural world and the then-prevailing norm of participating consciousness. There is nothing the least romantic about this. When the chief wrote, 'All things are connected. Whatever befalls the Earth befalls the sons of the Earth', he was referring to a universal truth and not a culturally specific one. When he rhetorically asked, 'What is it to say goodbye to the swift and the hunt, the end of living and the beginning of survival?' it was not merely platitude, for that is exactly what is at stake.

Many writers therefore appeal to us to see the Earth in its wholeness, indeed in its wholesomeness. We are in danger of overwhelming Earth if we consider ourselves disconnected from it. The human race is part of what has been called 'the implicate order'.

> Earth and life sciences . . . have . . . been torn apart by the
> ruthless dissection of science into separate and blinkered disciplines. Geologists have tried to persuade us that the Earth is just
> a ball of rock . . . . Life is merely an accident, a quiet passenger
> that happens to have hitched a ride on this rock ball in its
> journey through space and time. Biologists have been no better.
>
> (ibid: 11, 12)

It is this piecemeal approach, encouraged by the division of
human knowledge into subjects and disciplines, which has closed
our eyes to seeing Gaia, Earth, as one living system!

It is useful to note how this revised approach to awareness about
the earth is begining to link up with other areas of human
knowing. There is now, thankfully, a theology about ecology,
beautifully encapsulated in Thomas Berry's influential and much
quoted book *The Dream of the Earth* (1988). Berry is both an
American monastic and a cultural historian who has been deeply
influenced (as we noted in chapter 1 how others have been) by the
great Jesuit scientist Teilhard de Chardin. Berry (1988: 21) criticises our 'failure to think of ourselves as a species', and then
proceeds to demonstrate that the sages of all cultures, East and
West, have always addressed the deeper meanings of the 'relationship between the human community and the earth process' (ibid:
10); their wisdom is common and grew out of that engagement. He
then comments (ibid.: 20):

> Such consideration brings us back to the ancient sense of *Logos*
> in the Greek world, of *rita* in Hinduism, or *dharma* in Buddhism,
> of *tao, cheng,* and *jen* in the Chinese world. These are the ancient
> perceptions of the ordering, or the balancing, principles of the
> universe, the principles governing the interaction of all those
> basic forces constituting the earth process. To recognise and act
> according to those principles was the ultimate form of human
> wisdom.

The Columban priest Sean McDonagh in his book entitled *To Care
for the Earth; a Call to a New Theology* (1986) argues that we need to
tell children a new story about the universe, based upon what we
know from science but also imbued with the wonder and mythological colourings which are the natural offsprings of reverence.
The same view comes through in the book by physicist Brian
Swimme, *The Universe is a Green Dragon* (1989). Professor Paul

Davies, also a physicist, states in his influential book *God and the New Physics* (1983: 3) that 'no religion that bases its beliefs on demonstrably incorrect assumptions can expect to survive for very long'. Science, especially the new physics, is now impacting on what were formerly regarded as religious issues; it has 'actually advanced to the point where what were formerly religious questions can be seriously tackled' (ibid: ix), Davies says. As a result,

> a growing number of people believe that recent advances in fundamental science are more likely to reveal the deeper meaning of existence than [an] appeal to traditional religion.
>
> (ibid: 8)

So, he says, although it may seem bizarre to suggest it, science may offer 'a surer path to God than religion' does, largely because a sense of awe, respect, and wonder is now being generated through scientific discoveries about the cosmos.

All of this is consistent with perceptions about the cosmos which the Judaeo-Christian tradition developed. It suggested that the world-order is an incredible balance of harmonies described as *shalom*, a word variously translated as the peace, balance, fulfilment, order, well-being which pervades the universe. Anything which causes *shalom* to be violated, anything which produces disharmony or lack of balance, which diminishes the well-being of ourselves, or of others, or of any other creature which lives with us on the planet, anything like that is to be condemned, no matter by whom or by what it is caused. That violation is called *hamartia*, 'missing the mark', failing to be what we ought to be; the English translation is usually the inadequately understood word 'sin'. Essentially, then, any approach to knowledge, to our planet, to the cosmos and to ourselves which fails to show that we are all connected to and responsible for the whole is to be condemned, for it will create discord, division, and ultimately destruction. But the antithesis is *shalom*, and it shows in a wonder, awe, and reverence for the universe. Is it possible to ensure that these are the characteristics which underlie and interpenetrate all the curricula to which the present generation of schoolchildren will be exposed?

Thus Lovelock (1988: 225) poses the essential question, 'How can you and I live in harmony with Gaia?' After giving several useful, almost whimsical, suggestions, he makes this quite disturbing comment:

Any species (that is, any part of Gaia) that adversely affects the environment is doomed; but life goes on . . . Gaia is not purposefully antihuman, but so long as we continue to change the global environment against her preferences, we encourage our replacement with a more environmentally seemly species.

(ibid: 236)

Gaia will survive, although the human species may not! Lovelock's theory about life on earth seems to be working in the right direction, for we know intuitively that his feeling for Earth is the appropriate one. And it is now being espoused by some powerful friends.

In summary, then, to preserve this incredible life-form called planet Earth, parents, politicians, public and educators need to adopt quickly this new way of thinking about our world, and to construct with the rising generation a different frame of thinking, both about the world and also about our place in it. How can schools cope with that awesome demand?

ACTING OUT THE 'ONE-WORLD' THEME

One aspect of that task is not so difficult after all. The way one views the world is very much a matter of choice. It may not always seem deliberate, it is sometimes almost subconscious, somewhere below being a conscious act, it is frequently incidental, and it is often almost careless. Even so, day by day, minute by minute, we weave a tapestry of coherence for our lives, a web of beliefs, out of the incidental fabrics which we select from our ordinary experience. We actively construct the world through our categorising and ways of knowing, and we also contribute to a recovery of meaning and coherence by building a more adequate frame of reference for ourselves. So we can choose to counteract the sense of fragmentation, breakdown and loss of meaning which pervades post-modern cultures. An educative process which does not engage that essential basic human activity of creating meanings is not worth a great deal. One that actively promotes it can be a potent cultural force.

If that is the case, we need to understand an important characteristic about a living organism. It is social, says Lovelock; 'it exists in communities and collectives' (ibid: 18). Any living system, any life form, big or small, huge or minute, is a bundle or a collection, just as a living human being is a collection of organs and tissues – a heart, a kidney, lungs and so on – and any one of them can be kept alive independent of the body. We have shown that to be the case by means of transplants. So life is 'colligative', to use Lovelock's term, a collection of things bound or bonded together. The life-bundle regulates itself and keeps itself alive. The technical term for that property is 'homeostasis'. There is a kind of wisdom that controls the whole and maintains its livingness.

Berman's account of the way that Cartesian dualism and the Newtonian synthesis served to underpin the basic assumptions of the industrial world-view is one of the best available (Berman, 1981). He suggests that the recovery of 'participating consciousness' may be one of the routes to take toward achieving a more credible and sustainable epistemology. To a hard-headed scientist or an engineer this may seem a soft and imprecise notion, yet it is obvious that we are indeed all participants in a seamless web of relationships, both physical and otherwise (Dossey, 1982: 72–81). It is the narrow view which is of questionable legitimacy, not the wider one. The latter serves to reconnect us to the world which we have never left. Separation from the global process was simply an illusion fostered in part by viewing the world as though it was merely a thing, a machine.

Berman suggests that knowledge is not primarily cerebral (that is, formed in the brain) but sensuous, harvested through the use of all our senses and involving the whole range of human capacity. He suggests that when rationality is isolated and exaggerated, a radical narrowing of perception and possibility occurs. This constricting has accompanied both the scientific and the industrial revolutions. He writes:

> In the seventeenth century we threw out the baby with the bathwater. We discounted a whole landscape of inner reality because it did not fit in with the programme of industrial or mercantile exploitation and the directives of organised religion.
>
> (Berman, 1981: 132)

This process was certainly obscured by the immense practical success of rational intelligence and sheer technical power. But the human costs have been immense (Lasch, 1985; Postman, 1986). Even without the environmental costs, the subversion of human potential which this process has entailed would, on its own, make it necessary for us to renegotiate the Faustian bargain.

However, the way forward is not simply to reject instrumental rationality, empiricism or technology in any simple-minded way. That would be a major mistake. It is, rather, to situate each of them in a wider framework. This sounds reasonable enough, but the suggestion therein is radical, because instead of approaching the production, transmission and renewal of knowledge in conventional ways – through subjects, disciplines and specialities – we would need to begin from this wider and broader context of space and time. Participating consciousness, or direct perception of the reality of an interwoven cosmos, needs to be much more than a folk memory or a romantic dream. It should be an experienced reality.

A global perspective is the smallest frame within which to view human affairs. Anything less lacks the capacity to deal with the interconnectedness and systemicity that characterise the global system. Such a view would not have been possible a few short years ago, but with the development of ecological, systemic and holistic perspectives which we have touched on above, and by drawing upon a range of disciplines, it has rapidly become practicable. Furthermore, even at the admittedly low level of data, as distinct from knowledge or wisdom, such a view can be supported technically. For example, it is now possible for every classroom and home to have access via satellite to remote sensing on a real-time basis. That the supply of facilities like this has not yet happened is a consequence of the way that the agendas for info-tech (IT) have been subverted by vested interests and obsolete frameworks of understanding (Webster and Lambe in Weston, 1986: 58–79). As in so many other areas, a highly sophisticated technical capacity exists but the consciousness directing it remains preoccupied with power and control (Wilber, 1983c; Slaughter, 1987a). In other words, that consciousness is limited by an obsolete world-view.

It is for a similar reason that 'technical fixes' are not adequate to deal with social and ecological breakdown. We must begin to recognise that solutions are increasingly unavailable within the framework or category of knowing which allowed the problem to be experienced in the first place. We cannot create 'global systems consciousness' merely by installing computers or by fine-tuning the economy; it requires a recovery of human identity and purpose. The most significant step would be a qualitative shift of consciousness beyond the limitations of ego-obsessed life, beyond the tendency to 'look out for No. 1', and into concerns which are global, long-term and universal.

HIGHER AWARENESS, CRITICAL THINKING AND FORESIGHT

A persistent thread running throughout most cultures and spiritual traditions suggests that we are all and always immersed in a stream of knowing in a world brimming with immanent meaning. Since language cannot fully encompass or explain those realms, the descriptions often appear paradoxical. From within the desert of empiricism created by science, that is the end of the story. But human experience over many years and in diverse cultures suggests that in any particular context higher perceptions can exist which may not even be noticed from within lower categories of knowing and certainly cannot be explained by them. Thus, far from sustaining an adequate world-view, a worn-out rationalism can be a radically limited frame from which to read an interconnected world rich with textured truths. We deal with this issue more fully in the next chapter.

Suffice it to say here that higher awareness tends to be refined, peaceful, compassionate, and it is not under threat. It has existed in every age, and it survives in part because it does not need to consume the world nor destroy it. It recognises, with Siddhartha, that 'meaning and reality [are] not hidden somewhere behind things, they [are] in them, in all of them' (Hesse, 1951: 32). This is a pivotal insight which may help us to reassess the role of science, rationality and materialism in our lives and cultures. It is also congruent with the notion of the world as a community of species, each with its own inalienable right to existence. A recognition that such shaping insights exist may not become widespread quickly, but they can certainly energise the here-and-now. Indeed, they may suggest the route for a journey which leads up and out of the abyss toward new stages of development, personally and for the human community.

If, therefore, we are to get a clear grasp of the fundamental causes of our global predicament, then we will be alert to the highest insights available to humankind. But we will also need to look beneath the surface of everyday structures and events to those underlying frameworks of meaning which powerfully shape our views of the world. At this deeper level the focus is not so much on trends, events and issues as on values, meanings, ideologies and assumptions. From this perspective we might consider the green-house effect not simply as a result of carbon dioxide and other emissions in the atmosphere but as a consequence of the dominance of instrumental rationality within the industrial world-view, and the way that value-set manifests itself in human behaviours. The earlier mode of rationality is basically about getting things done; it concentrates on means, but it tends to be silent about ends. That is why Lewis Mumford was able to say of modern weapons systems that the means were rational but the ends were entirely mad. Critical thinking is therefore extremely important. It does not simply mean 'to criticise'. Rather, it points to the ability to see more deeply. This is crucial. Otherwise we may readily be dazzled by the bright display of technical surfaces, quite overlooking the shaping realities beneath.

Similarly, foresight is not just a question of understanding possible consequences and avoiding them; it is also about the need to change the inherited assumptions and modes of perception and belief which gave rise to those consequences. Another way of saying this is that we are learning the hard way that the Western world-view is unsustainable. We have suggested that it is being replaced quite rapidly by an awareness of how connected the world is, how directly human action causes ripple effects throughout the fabric of life and nature, how dangerous it is to allow pockets of people or individual nations to engage in activities which affect the health of the whole planet.

In this chapter, then, we have argued that global consciousness is a factor in the new world-view. It is not a merely pretty idea, but a premise upon which to base action and behaviours, and to illuminate discourse. Higher awareness, critical thinking and foresight are themselves interwoven with, and supportive of, global sensibility. Each is part of the newly developing paradigm. It will become part of the framework which everyone, and especially young people, will use to interpret the world as we perceive it.

Chapter 4

Beyond scientific materialism
Accepting other categories of knowing

The existing political economy generates fresh material demands with each new level of production; the escalating demands intensify the search for further advances in operational techniques. Other dimensions of possible experience are repressed under the weight of this self-defeating enterprise.

William Leiss, *The Limits to Satisfaction*, 1976

What we take to be the present necessarily refers back and forward in time. Our reality grows out of past history, but is powerfully shaped too by what we believe about the future. Similarly, our decisions, the technologies we collectively employ, the ideologies and ends we pursue all frame and condition the world of our descendants. In other words, whatever we do, we cannot be uninvolved. This is immensely important for such a view leads to a deep sense of historical process and connectedness in space and time.

Richard Slaughter, *The Dinosaur and the Dream*, 1985

In the first chapter we pointed out that there are three important strands affecting the process of reworking our view about the world. The three impact on each other, but it is important to comprehend each of them because in this decade they will influence just about everything the human community does. Chapter 2 considered the first of the three, the fundamental shift occurring in economics and the world of work. In chapter 3 we discussed the new globalism and 'participating consciousness'.

The third major feature of the changing world-views is the shift in attitude about modern science, and what constitutes knowledge. Again, there is a wide range of writings on this topic and while we cannot pretend to deal comprehensively with it here, it is important to recognise not only the nature of the shift but also to appreciate how fundamental it is. We need therefore to summarise the historical development which has led us to this point.

EDUCATION AND THE INDUSTRIAL WORLD-VIEW

According to some observers, our present difficulties began with the onset of the scientific revolution, the so-called Age of Enlightenment, when the medieval view was supplanted: 'The notion of an organic, living and spiritual universe was replaced by that of the world as a machine, and the world-machine became the dominant metaphor of the modern era.' (Capra, 1982: 38)

So enquiry became scientific, reductionist. We made progress with knowledge by breaking any phenomenon down into its component bits. As we studied and analysed all those pieces, we would build up logically and systematically, by synthesis, an understanding about the whole. By adopting that same, empirical, piece-by-piece approach to every aspect of reality we made spectacular progress. We applied the approach to Newtonian Physics, biology and living organisms, systems theory, medicine, psychology, even to economics and political systems.

One of the most significant first figures in the so-called Scientific Movement was Francis Bacon (1561–1626), a contemporary of Shakespeare. Bacon put forward the proposition that scientific knowledge was cumulative, and that it was built up over time by systematic, methodical work in a process called induction. His 'new scientific method involved a concentration upon facts, not theology or opinion or sophisticated argumentation' (Brown H., 1986: 5–7). It was a landmark development, for until that time, scientific development was held in rein by whether it conformed with the orthodox theology of the time. The Copernican revolution and the excommunication of Galileo from the Church had occurred because while direct observation and empirical evidence had suggested that the sun, not the earth, was the centre of the universe, the scientific evidence was ruled out of order because it ran counter to prevailing theology. Since the time of the scientific enlightenment and thus over the past three hundred years, there developed a rift between science and Western religion.

Capra (1982: 37) explains the fundamental difference in the world-view prior to 1500 and that of the subsequent three centuries:

Before 1500 the dominant world view in Europe, as well as in most other civilizations, was organic. People lived in small cohesive communities and experienced nature in terms of organic relationships, characterized by the inter-dependence of spiritual and material phenomena. . . . The scientific framework of this organic world view rested on two authorities – Aristotle and the Church. . . . The nature of medieval science was very different from that of contemporary science.

Once the scientific method was established, our ways of knowing, and especially the way knowledge is accumulated and stored, changed dramatically. The results are seen in retrospect to characterise 'the Scientific Revolution, the Enlightenment, and the Industrial Revolution'. We need to note that a new way of knowing has a ripple effect. Social patterns change, the configuration of towns and cities, occupational patterns, education and philosophical inquiry, what we read and where we travel are all affected.

In the past three hundred years, then, we have been driven by the belief in the scientific method as the only valid approach to knowledge; the view of the universe as a mechanical system composed of elementary building blocks; the view of life in society as a competitive struggle; and the belief in unlimited material progress to be achieved through economic and technological growth.

(Capra, 1982: 12)

Every one of these elements, Capra points out, has been shown to be 'severely limited and in need of radical revision'. There are several aspects of this world-view which are so familiar that they tend to fall into the category of taken-for-granted and have therefore not been subjected to incisive questioning until recently. Changing any one of them will force revisions to our accepted ways of acting and thinking. Changing all of them, and simultaneously, will cause a revolution! And that is what we are facing at the present time.

The characteristics of the scientific framework are well known; the following list is based upon Willis Harman's analysis (Harman, 1988: 29–33).

Reductionism The way to understanding is to break things down into their component parts, to separate them. We can then examine each of the parts in detail, and by building up our knowledge of the individual pieces we will come to an under-standing of the whole. Science is therefore reductionist; scientists become specialists, finding out all they can with ever increasing sophistication about particular phenomena or subdisciplines.

Positivism The major defensible way in which we can extend our knowledge about the universe is through empirical methods, by relying solely on what we can observe. By experimentation and measurement, especially by relying upon the physical senses and the technology which extends them, we arrive at verifiable truth. Only what can be verified is trustworthy and admissible as knowledge.

Materialism The empiricist works only with what is substantial and real, insisting on evidence which can be examined. Even what we descibe as consciousness or awareness can be understood by analysing the physical and chemical processes in the body.

Objectivity There is a clear distinction between the objective world, which any observer can perceive and which all observers will read in the same way, and subjectivity which is limited to the privacy of one's own brain and consciousness. What is objective is reliable; what is subjective can be dismissed unless the subjectivities of several people confirm each other and therefore verify (or give face validity to) an objective conclusion.

Rationality Reason is the indispensible partner to empiricism. The application of reasoning, rigorous logic, dispassionate (and therefore value-free, or unemotional) rationality, especially when based upon observed phenomena, is the only safe method where-by to advance knowledge. As Goldberg (1983: 17) put it, 'the right way to approach knowledge is with a rigorous interchange of reason and systematically acquired (sensory) experience'.

Quantitative analysis It stands to reason, then, that qualitative properties are best reduced to quantitative ones, to properties which can be weighed, measured, rendered objective and assessable.

Anti-enchantment Goldberg (ibid.: 18) argues that 'scientism', an unnecessary belief in science's one best way, has devoured other fields of knowing.

> Flushed with success, the juggernaut of science gobbled up terrain formerly held by philosophy, metaphysics, theology, and cultural tradition. We sought to apply the methods that worked

so well in the material realm to answer questions about the psyche, the spirit, and society. Through experimentation and the application of reason . . . it was assumed we would come to know the secrets of the universe and learn how to live. To accomplish this, we set out to perfect the objective tools of knowing. . . . Over time, our organisations and educational institutions made scientism the *sine qua non* of knowing, the model for how to think.

In summary, then, the rational-empirical had triumphed over all else, and it held sway for about three hundred years.

As Ken Wilber (1983: 23) and others have pointed out, a scheme for 'knowing' which was limited to so small a base and which ruled as inadmissible anything which was not material was bound in the end to become a nonsense. 'In effect', he says, 'the sole criterion of truth came to be the empiric criterion – that is to say, a sensorimotor test by the eye of flesh (or its extension) based upon measurement'. Thus, Wilber comments, 'we simply note that nonfleshy (i.e. non-physical, non-material) came to mean unreal'. He quotes the philosopher Whitehead; 'this position on the part of the scientists was pure bluff, if one may credit them with [actually] believing their own statements'. Wilber goes on: 'Science was becoming scientism, known also as positivism, known also as scientific materialism, and *that* was a bluff of the part playing the whole.'

This is a crucial point. The scientific method has advanced the world's knowledge enormously, especially over recent decades; its achievements are not to be devalued. It is not that science is wrong, but rather that it should not and cannot exert a universal and exclusive claim on the generation and validation of knowledge.

It follows that the claim of science to being objective, value-free and entirely dispassionate in its orientations and methods is no longer universally tenable. The Harvard sociologist Robert K. Merton was able to enunciate in 1973 these four fundamental principles of scientific inquiry (cited in Brown, 1986: 133-4):

- *Universalism*: science is international and culturally unbiassed, independent of the racial, political or value stance of the researcher.
- *Communalism*: scientific knowledge is public knowledge, to be shared, to be critically examined by peers, and is not to be kept 'secret'. For this reason, the scientist is expected to publish the

outcomes of her or his research, and to encourage the critical analysis of those who know the field.

* *Disinterestedness*: the results of one's research ought to be openly and honestly reported, and are not to be manipulated, changed, or made malleable for personal profit or to serve political priorities, and are not to be subjugated to religious, social or ideological purposes.

* *Organised scepticism*: nothing is accepted on authority, but all is subject to a variety of critical responses. The consideration of a matter from the standpoint of deliberate disbelief is the only credible way to test whether a proposition is robust and trustworthy. In fact, belief systems are suspect because they tend to distort the truth.

Commendable though these four principles may seem to be, we are now aware that none of Merton's norms apply in a pure form, or in all circumstances, none of them is universal. Scientific inquiry emerges from a social/cultural context which has many common biases and blind spots. Were it otherwise, then we would find it difficult to explain why military and private industry research accounts for about 90 per cent of the world's research endeavour, why medical research focuses disproportionately on the diseases of the developed world, and why it is affluent societies which pay for and control the research agenda.

What develops from this approach is a fragmented, fractured view of the cosmos and of our part in it. We encourage people so much in the 'bits' approach that they do not identify with the whole. How else can we explain the expenditure of huge sums on armaments while children starve? Why do industries concentrate on producing materials and their own private riches with so little concern about the pollution of streams and atmosphere resulting from their own waste? How else can we explain destruction parading as growth; consumption being called development; starvation produced by multinational agribusiness corporations; health and the prevention of illness being treated as though they are separate enterprises? How is it that while about half of the world's scientists are engaged in warfare-related research, and while world military spending is more than one billion dollars a day, one person in three on the planet does not have access to safe drinking water? This is indeed the dark side of growth and the approaches to knowledge-production.

One of the most profound reasons for questioning science is that it has begun to recoil on itself, producing counter-intuitive findings and some developments which will not fit into the tidy scientific paradigm. Not least is this the case with the purest of the pure sciences, physics. Harman (1988: 106) comments, 'The ultimate triumph of reductionist physics is to demonstrate the *necessity* of a new paradigm which goes beyond reductionist science'. 'To put it bluntly', the physicist Capra says in another place, 'scientists do not deal with truth; they deal with limited and approximate descriptions of reality' (Capra, 1982: 33).

THE WAY SCHOOLS TREAT KNOWLEDGE

Not surprisingly because of its origins, the whole education establishment operates in that same bits-and-pieces approach which characterised the scientific method. For example, to construct the curriculum of secondary and primary schools, and also in universities, we break human knowledge down into disciplines, subjects and courses; and we allocate those specialisations to people who are trained in particular areas of knowledge. We make the assumption that the parts will add up to a coherent whole, and that the whole is indeed merely the sum of the parts.

The important point here is that schools faithfully reproduce this distorted world-view, both in what they teach and also in the very ways in which the learning process is conceived of, organised, and delivered. It permeates the texture of education. Its influence is visible in the artifically produced competition in schools, in an infatuation with marks and grades, in the scrabble for status created by hierarchies of schools, in the reduction of pupils to statistics, in the creation of 'experts', and in the near-absence of any credible futures perspective.

It has to be acknowledged that this way of understanding the world has led to some of the most remarkable achievements of the human race, and also to some of its most deplorable depravities. For the twenty-first century we had better discover quickly how schools in particular can sponsor a different orientation: in place of fragmentation, wholeness and connectedness; in place of devastation and disease, health and balance. But before this transformation can happen, the educational enterprise will need to regain the initiative from economists, accountants and bureaucrats.

DIFFERENT WAYS OF KNOWING

Simply stated, then, we are moving beyond the approaches to the generation of knowledge which have been regarded as standard for past decades, widening the window, as it were. What kind of a framework is emerging to replace the one which has been taken for granted for three centuries?

Various writers have tried to demonstrate the wider perspective which is now gaining acceptance, and to make their explanations accessible, they have tried to present schemas for thinking which include but go beyond the limits of the framework of scientific materialism. They admit that their new frameworks are speculative and incomplete, but in trying to understand their search for a better explanation we can show how the paradigm is enlarging our vision or 'ways of knowing'.

In his *Guide for the Perplexed* (1977), the economist Schumacher suggests that our ancestors' view of the world was broadly hierarchical, made up of four distinct levels – mineral, plant, animal and human. If one begins at the lowest level and moves upward, then one clearly sees emergent qualities. In moving from the level of plants to humans, for example, the qualities that emerge are consciousness and self-awareness. Between each level there is an 'ontological discontinuity' or qualitative difference in the level of being. This means that the distinguishing qualities of a higher level cannot be reduced to a lower level, though they must be congruent with it. Thus life is different from and greater than non-life, consciousness is different from and greater than vegetative life and self-awareness is different from and greater than unreflective consciousness. In other words, 'there are differences in kind, and not simply in degree, between the powers of life, consciousness and self-awareness' (ibid.: 30).

It follows that while in some sense the higher incorporates the lower, from the viewpoint of the lower the higher is always mysterious, or occluded, or beyond understanding. Mineral, which is supposedly lifeless, cannot regard vegetable, which is living; vegetable cannot know animal, which has consciousness, and animal cannot grasp human reflexivity. Hence the 'rules' of existence on any level are level-specific and the higher the level, the greater the complexity and the more new rules will apply. If this schema is followed, each level is open-ended above and below. Thus, according to Schumacher, 'the most important insight that follows from the contemplation of the four great Levels of Being [is that] at the level of man there is no discernable limit or ceiling'. In his view, self-awareness is 'a power of unlimited potential' (ibid.: 48).

In much the same way as Schumacher grappled with hierarchical levels of knowing, Fraser in his major work *Time As Conflict* (1978) tries to show that time itself can be understood in a more structured way. The Newtonian or scientific models tend to depict time simply, as a linear movement through events from past to future. Fraser, on the other hand, suggests that time can be understood at several levels, each corresponding to a particular world of reference (or *Umwelt* to use his term). The atemporal *Umwelt* is a world of reference without considering time at all, one of undifferentiated existence; it is 'a universe of purely relativistic energy' (ibid.: 30) where nothing is identified with the features of time, no succession, duration or interval. The prototemporal *Umwelt* is a step nearer to the one we recognise, but space and time are not clearly separated; instead, 'histories and group actions. . . are interchangeable, as are things and events. Events are 'connected' through a kind of controlled randomness, (and) hence 'probability is the paradigm of physical law' (ibid.: 50). Fraser then proposes an *eotemporal* world or *Umwelt,* a world of cosmic time, of eons, a frame of reference involving 'pure succession, with no direction of time and no nowness' (ibid.: 60). This is the world or universe as studied by astronomers, cosmologists and theorists of general relativity.

Fraser maintains that our notions of 'futurity, pastness and presentness' cannot be derived from a world which is this vast and inanimate. 'No physical process', he writes, 'can determine *Umwelts* higher than the pure succession of the eotemporal.' We need life and mind in order to do that. In other words, higher integrative levels have their own qualities which are only partially determined by a base in the physical world. Thus biotemporality is the *Umwelt* which identifies the world of life. It is here that 'the necessary inner coordination of living matter inserts a meaningful present into the pure succession of the eotemporal world' (ibid.: 80). It gives time and meanings a 'local habitation and a name', to use Shakespeare's phrase. Furthermore, it is life which gives us the awareness that time has direction; 'no arrow of time can become explicit except through the autonomy of life', declares Fraser (ibid.: 90). It is the 'totality of life' which creates and defines what is the collective present.

But life itself supports mind, particularly in human beings, and it leads Fraser to suggest that the highest *Umwelt*, the highest frame of reference, is nootemporal. This is the familiar world of culture, of human meaning, of imagination and the symbolic trans-formation of experience. Thus the mental present is established at the peak of Fraser's hierarchy; order and unity are induced by 'that artificial narrowing of our interest which we call attention' (ibid.: 119).

Some of Fraser's comments about this scheme both echo and extend what has already been said in connection with Schumacher's view. First, 'each of the major levels must be described in different, level-specific languages'. Second, 'the laws of each integrative level leave certain regions of their world un-regarded, and hence undetermined. It is from the undetermined regions that the regularities of the next higher level arise'. Third, 'level-specific laws are unpredictable from *Umwelts* lower than the one to which they apply and are inexpressible in terms of lower languages' (ibid.: 26). Fraser's ideas help to explain why more advanced stages of consciousness and being tend to appear obscure or mysterious, and why a line or method of inquiry which fits one area may not be transferable or even appropriate for another area.

The same notion is inherent in the analysis of Willis Harman in *Global Mind Change* (1988). In a section entitled 'Choose your metaphysic', Harman argues that 'a society's basic experiencing of reality shapes its science', that from time to time society adopts 'other views . . . seen through other cultural windows', and that the developing trans-modern view 'may be quite different from our own – and equally correct' (ibid.: 33–4). He then proposes 'three basically different kinds of implicit metaphysic' which we can use to explain what we perceive reality to be, pointing out that the first, the familiar 'matter-energy' approach which makes the 'positivist assumption' that dealing with the 'measurable world' is 'the only way we can learn', fails to give adequate explanations of some of the findings thrown up by science itself. He suggests that his third metaphysic requires a 'fundamental change' which may 'seem as outrageous a proposition as the heliocentric universe did to many in early seventeenth-century Europe' (ibid.: 35).

It is significant, too, that Habermas, working from a different discipline base, happens upon the same kind of schema to explain 'human cognitive interests'. Habermas thereby provides an interpretive framework which permits us to reflect on social processes in a new and penetrating way. In this account, he invents a category called the technical interest, which relates to 'work' and the empirical/analytic sciences concerned with production and control (that is, the application of technical rules to instrumental problems). A second category, the practical interest, concerns human interaction. Here the concern is not with control, nor with technical processes, but with the communication and understanding among people which are grounded in language and culture. The main concern is to clarify the conditions which make for clear and unobstructed communication between the participating subjects. These are seen as tasks of interpretation which require hermeneutic (interpretive) skills. The third and 'highest' category is the emancipatory interest, which relates to questions of power and the universal drive for emancipation and freedom of action (Habermas, 1971).

Habermas does not attempt to denigrate the technical interest *per se* since our civilisation is dependent upon the maintenance of effective and efficient technical processes. Rather, he is set against its over-extension into areas which are illegitimate for it, such as when decisions about a new technology are made on the basis of 'Can it be done?' rather than 'Should it be done?' A major concern in the area of the practical interest (the second category) is that there are so many factors (such as power, ideology, marketing and direct exploitation) from the third category which impede, even prevent, true communication from taking place between individuals and groups. The issue at stake, then, is that of defining the conditions under which communication can be optimised. This is clearly not a technical question but one which relates to the richer and more complex world of human intersubjectivity. (We may note in passing that, contrary to what the proponents of 'artifical intelligence' would have us believe, the term 'communication' may only have a residual meaning when applied at the technical level.) The emancipatory interest is engaged in defining the conditions within which people can create an authentic existence for themselves, and thus forces us into a critique of domination, repression, mystification and institutional inertia.

Habermas's scheme is less clear-cut than those of Schumacher, Fraser, and Harman but the same general features can be observed in all of them:

- distinct levels with different rules appropriate for each level;
- open-endedness;
- simple procedures for detecting category errors;
- an in-built counter to reductionism (the inverse logic of assuming that the lower subsumes the higher).

Such consistency among these writers is reassuring, especially since they come at the problem out of different disciplines, for not only does it demonstrate a similar uneasiness with the prevailing frame of reference, with what until now has been taken for granted, but it also suggests the possibility of broad agreement about the shape of the solution.

Perhaps the person who has put the new framework for thinking in terms which are most accessible is Ken Wilber, particularly in his book *Eye to Eye* (1983), significantly subtitled 'The Quest for the New Paradigm'. Wilber has probably done as much as anyone to re-establish the grounds for a comprehensive paradigm of knowing and being, and in doing so he has covered an enormous amount of ground by way of developmental psychology, anthropology, consciousness and religion. In each of these areas he found evidence of the same hierarchical structuring and distinct levels which characterise the writers we have already cited. His simplest account of ways of knowing has three main levels.

Wilber takes his lead from St Bonaventure who distinguished between an eye of flesh ('by which we perceive the external world of space, time, and objects'), an eye of reason ('by which we attain a knowledge of philosophy, logic and the mind itself') and an eye of contemplation ('by which we rise to a knowledge of transcendent realities'). He comments that, though the wording of this account is Christian, 'similar ideas can be found in every major school of traditional psychology, philosophy and religion' (Wilber, 1983: 3).

The eye of flesh corresponds to the gross world experienced through the senses. It is an empirical way of knowing of which number is the paradigmatic method and empirical science the product. It operates upon the realm of nature. The eye of reason is more subtle and it corresponds to the inner world of ideas, images, meanings and concepts. This is a way of knowing whose method is theory, whose subject is history and whose goal is philosophical and psychological insight. The eye of contemplation is more subtle still. Its method is direct perception of suchness; its goal is spiritual wisdom and its realm is transcendence.

Later in his book, Wilber amplifies his schema into three modes of knowing, three ways in which we develop ideas about the cosmos which encloses us. He calls the data dealt with in the three modes sensibilia, intelligibilia, and transcendelia. Because the classifications are helpful once they are understood, it is worthwhile considering them in more detail. The fact is that these three domains are known to us, and, since the dawn of time, the human species has been acquiring knowledge in all three domains and recognising its impressive consistency, across time, race, religion, culture and class. If ever anything has been verified and found to be authentic, this coherence in human experiencing must be it.

Sensibilia is that familiar zone in which science has traditionally operated. This domain deals with sensory experience. Its raw material is empirical data, observed and analysed by means of the scientific method. The knowledge derived from this domain we recognise as the 'hard sciences'. The mode of inquiry in this domain is a monologue. It requires only the detached observer, collecting data alone and subjecting them to rigorous, rational analysis. Verification is essentially instrumental; if the theory 'works', then it is valid.

Intelligibilia is of a different order from sensibilia. In this domain, comments Wilber (1983: 47), 'the "things" we are looking at . . . are *thoughts* – their structure and their form – as they immediately display themselves to the inward mental eye'. The raw materials are therefore reported, for they cannot be physically observed by someone else as is the case with sensibilia. Thus the mode of inquiry is mental and phenomenological (an experience which is related and described). The domain deals with the analysis of one's thought processes, with symbolics (things or experiences which carry deeper meanings), with language and linguistics. Intelligibilia therefore give rise to the disciplines of philosophy, psychology, and history. The processes for the domain are clinical (rather than empirical). Importantly too, the mode of inquiry requires dialogue (where sensibilia rest upon monologue), for to come to terms with the data, the one experiencing them has to talk them to another person; there is no other way to make the data accessible. Thus the mode requires communication and interaction (where sensibilia required only detached observation, documenting what one 'sees'). The verification is intuitive, a coherence born of similarity in interpretation. As Wilber (ibid.: 59) points out, 'we have been producing a decently coherent and fairly unified view of human psychological growth and development' which is essentially agreed upon.

Transcendelia occupy a domain which has been acknowledged by countless generations of human beings who testify to deeper perceptions and experiences which cannot be tamed by either the sensibilia or the intelligibilia domains. In this domain the mode of inquiry is meditative or contemplative, for the data are derived from 'transcendental perception' which 'cannot be perceived with the mental or the sensory eyes'. Included in this domain are experiences described as religious, spiritual, or mythological, the perceptions which come from altered states of consciousness. This area, then, is open only to those who are sufficiently 'developed' in terms of transcendental perception to comprehend the data. Interestingly, however, the data are verifiable, for they are communal, shared, repeatable. The saints of all ages and all cultures tend to speak a similar language, attesting to a commonality of (albeit) rare experiences, and, while admitting the inadequacy of language to describe the ineffable, they fall back on the same imagery, the same symbols, the same archetypes, which Wilber admits constitute 'a sound and valid transcendental methodology' (ibid.: 61).

Wilber's analysis here is brilliant, for he clarifies the problem of category error. There is consistency and logic in each domain, each has its own mode of operation and inquiry, each has aspects that are appropriate to that domain and to that domain alone. The key problem arises when we try to extract inappropriate data from the wrong domain, or when we apply the methods of inquiry and analysis from one domain to another domain.

Several points stand out here. The first is that contemplation cannot be reduced to reason, nor reason to the senses. Each is ontologically distinct. To take the lower for the higher is to commit a category error. To put it differently, the truth of ideas cannot be seen by the senses, the reality of direct perception cannot be 'seen' by reason – or as Wilber puts it (ibid.: 10), 'sensation, reason and contemplation disclose their own truths in their own realms and any time one eye tries to see for another eye, blurred vision results'.

There could not be a more concise critique of industrialised culture than this, for such a culture, based on the simplifications of the Newtonian synthesis, validates number and theory and discounts direct perception. It commits a double category error and obscures the most crucial area for future development, explaining why the culture has lost its coherence and why many attempted solutions to problems do not work. As noted above, there are very often no effective solutions at the level at which they are experienced. It is often only by understanding the broader structure and the creative potential within the problem or conflict that a conscious decision can be made to transcend the level upon which the problem first manifests.

In summary, then, each of the writers we have cited covers broadly comparable ground; Fraser stops at the nootemporal level, believing that there is no higher level from which to contemplate it (Fraser, 1987: 248–9). Similarly, while Schumacher explicitly states that 'no upper limit' can be discerned at the human level, Habermas stops at the emancipatory interest, completely missing the primacy of contemplation. Yet this is just what one would expect, given the narrowness of the Newtonian paradigm and the rapid development of frameworks derived from it. When Ruth Benedict (1935: 2) observed that 'no man ever looks at the world with pristine eyes . . . ; he sees it edited by a definite set of customs and institutions and ways of thinking', she could hardly have foreseen how savage the editing could become. Yet in spite of the very many extensions of view made possible through science and technology, they are essentially 'horizontal', limited to their own domain. A narrow, instrumental view of the world has never been fully convincing, nor could it be when it omits the very pinnacles of knowing and being.

Taken together, these writers establish a strong case for re-establishing the qualitative dimension of human experience. It is what Berman (1981) calls the 're-enchantment of the world'. It is also described by McDonagh (1986: 77–8) as freeing the human community 'from the grip of the machine metaphor' and developing 'a new story or myth of the emergence of the Earth', based upon 'modern ways of knowing'. McDonagh admits that the raw material for the story comes from science, but it will be truly a revolutionary story and confirms, without a shadow of doubt, that the universe 'does not run on mechanistic principles. . . . It shows the old story (of the past three hundred years) to be shallow in comparison to the new one's magnificent span of twenty billion years. It also tells us that unless we abandon mechanistic science and technology we place in jeopardy the future florescence of this beautiful Earth'.

Here, then, are the makings of a different paradigm, which could also be a new set of constructs for designing education. It is one which:

- provides an explicit basis for superseding reductionism;
- provides a constructive framework from which to address the underlying sources of global problems;
- suggests a way to examine the taken-for-granted and to move to a more fluid, open and inclusive awareness;
- explains why many phenomena appear mysterious in their original terms (since higher integrative levels tend to appear mysterious or paradoxical in the language and view of the lower) and therefore are not addressed;
- helps us recognise the positive potential within conflict and crisis;
- suggests how interdisciplinarity may be a structural necessity within fields like education and curriculum studies; and
- reveals how the future options for western societies can be inspired by shifts toward higher levels of integration and consciousness.

This schema does not wipe out empirical methods of inquiry, but it does show that it is unnecessary to be limited to that form of inquiry, and it does make admissible a much wider range of human experiencing and 'knowledge' production.

MOVING INTO THE NEW PARADIGM

To sum up: the discussion in the three previous chapters has led by three routes to an important synthesis. *Superseding the industrial and materialist framework* leads to new ways of depicting the world of work, and new developments within politics, economics and social behaviours. Continuing in the old paradigm leads to social problems such as poverty traps, crime born of despair and social dislocation, large-scale unemployment, nihilism, short-termism, pessimism. *Superseding the false duality about human beings and their environment* leads to a new appreciation of the one-ness of the 'earth community', and saves us from the disabling, unthinking actions which are in the process of destroying life on earth. *Superseding scientific materialism* puts knowledge production into a new and wider framework, one which includes science but which saves us from being bluffed by a part pretending to be the whole. It opens up dimensions to human experience which are the most ennobling and transcendent.

Synthesising all three of these major shifts into an integrated new picture reinvests education with an awesome, heady mission. What precisely can teachers and parents do with the new vision? We turn to that consideration in the next chapters.

Chapter 5

What will become of schools?

The integrity of a living system or a social system resides in its capacity to maintain its present. It is impossible to maintain a viable social-global present unless it is made a part of the flow of history. But of whose history? The people of the earth are at war to decide whose interpretation of the past is going to shape the future of mankind. The ethos that will eventually conquer the minds of people will be the one that succeeds in creating a framework of historical understanding for which a believable and inspiring future may be constructed.

Fraser, J. T. Time the Familiar Stranger, 1987

If education and schooling are to adapt appropriately to the twenty-first century, they will have to develop along lines which break with the earlier paradigm. As teachers and schools begin to focus upon that role which involves some social reconstruction and a more adequate framework, they will build on the trends which we have discussed above. Their activities will need to be based on a non-reductionist world-view, to include a cultural analysis which includes but goes beyond critique, and to draw up a set of educational goals and responsibilities which match *human* needs.

It is not possible to predict the future of social systems in great detail, but it seems obvious that education will have to reject merely instrumental and reductionistic approaches. The all-important, non-quantifiable dimensions of educational work cannot remain subordinated to technical, economic or purely rationalistic imperatives. The educational philosophy essential for the twenty-first century will need to balance social/economic requirements with individual and cultural ones.

What is to become, then, of schools and schooling? An important premise must be stated at the outset. A new paradigm widens or redraws frameworks but it rarely demolishes what existed before; it simply incorporates those elements into a more embracing perceptual frame. Thus when Copernicus proposed that the heavenly bodies revolved around the sun and not the earth, the new frame accepted the notions of the circular motions of the 'stars'. In subsequent centuries, of course, neither explanation has been shown to be accurate – orbital paths are elliptical, not circular; planets of the sun are not stars; the solar system is only part of the universe and not at its centre; and so on. But each new paradigm subsumes what preceded it. In the same way, schooling for the twenty-first century will build on what we already know to be valid about learning, expanding the canvas rather than obliterating the part of the picture already painted on it.

If schools are to incorporate the ideas discussed in chapters 2, 3 and 4, we must consider first how schools can be turned into 'post-bureaucratic' organisations. We then must understand how school culture can be used as a conveyor of a new world-view. Finally we explore the imagery and metaphors which might be used to embody a more adequate world-view.

BUILDING ONTO THE EXISTING SHAPE OF SCHOOLS

The problems involved in bringing about educational change should not be underestimated, but one thing in our favour is that we already know what makes a good school. The topic has been extensively researched over the past two decades, and what has been discovered looks reliable largely because it is not spectacularly new. We know that:

Good schools have clear educational aims, which apply to the behaviours of staff no less than to students. Good schools target learning outcomes. They believe that every student can learn and is willing to learn. An attitude of success permeates the whole school. Good schools are constantly on the search for a better way of doing things. They do not just talk about good ideas; they go out and practise them. A good school has a good Principal who is an educator rather than merely a manager, a person whose interest is primarily in teaching and learning. Good schools concentrate on teaching and learning. They understand that their core task is educating, they devote more classroom time to that task, their teachers direct their energy to academic learning, they test regularly for achievement, they set homework and follow up to see that it is done. There is a school-wide, systematic, regular assessment program for the school. Good schools 'maintain an orderly and safe environment' for learning. In good schools, it is safe for a student to be curious, to play with ideas, to experiment and to make mistakes. Good schools do not burden either their students or their staff so heavily that time for enrichment, time to reflect, time to participate in recreation or artistic or professional or other educational pursuits are crowded out of the program. To quote Clark, Lotto and Astuto (1989: 183), 'Good schools are good places to live and work (in), for everybody'.

(Beare, 1989b)

So we can recognise what good schooling is like, its characteristics isolated by more than twenty years of systematic research and inquiry. In consequence, we know that there are already in many countries thousands of good schools which conform with these requirements, and which are ready to adapt to the new paradigm.

We also know a great deal about about how to run such schools. Many of those who manage the education enterprise have sophisticated training in management, policymaking and planning, and they are handling a wider range of functions than was the case even ten years ago. For example, if one aggregates the salary bill in any normally sized school of, say, about forty staff members, the capital value of the buildings and equipment, the costs of maintenance and supplies, and its other recurrent expenditures, it becomes immediately apparent that a significantly large school is not only a enterprise, but that it is usually the largest business enterprise in the town or suburb where it is located. It is often the municipality's biggest company and it occupies the largest piece of its real estate. So the managers of these enterprises should be respected for what they really are. They are among the most highly skilled and qualified executives in the community. Furthermore, the enterprise they administer is usually much more complicated than other local businesses, largely because its purposes are more complex, more public, and more politically sensitive. Planning a new school enterprise incorporating the characteristics of the new paradigm is a task for which ready-made managers exist.

We also know about running school systems. At the state, provincial, or national levels, the education 'corporation' is huge by any standards. An education system and individual schools are very complex enterprises, and, by and large, they are being very ably run. Although education itself is an intricate process, those involved in its management have sophisticated knowledge of it. For example, educators know a great deal about assessment and grading, far outstripping the public's comprehension of the process. They know about curriculum design, and learning processes, about technology in the classroom and so on. Thus although the education enterprise is a highly sophisticated one, there are some very knowledgeable operators within it. This picture is repeated around the world.

No country or government is likely to set aside the accumulated expertise of those responsible for providing education, and we do not advocate that course of action in this book. Rather, it is prudent to reconstruct education from the existing materials, but making adaptations which suit the paradigm shift we have explored in earlier chapters.

Beyond the sophisticated knowledge and expertise we already have about schooling, we already know a great deal about what the next decade, and even the next century, will be like. A great number of the trends have been so well documented and described in print that they ought to have been thoroughly digested by now. Nor are the broad implications for young people hard to discern. But, since we are not using our foresight capacities to the full, we tend to notice them later rather than sooner, and often when it is almost too late to react to them positively.

For example, we know a great deal about the kind of world which the children now in school are about to inherit. To take one case, figures from the 1989 United Nations world population survey showed that in spite of world development, family planning, and birth control, the planet's population is still climbing by 90 million people every year; in other words, the world's population adds to itself more than the population of the British Isles each year. At this rate, one hundred years from now the world's population will have tripled. Consider the consequences of that one statistic in terms of food, the use of electricity and power, global pollution, the disposal of waste, government, and so on – and remember that we are talking about the living space and the life span of the children who are in elementary schools *now*.

On this evidence, because it is the poor, black and developing countries which lack the means of birth control, only about one in every ten live births in the world will be of European stock. We therefore know much of what students in school today need to learn so that they can thrive in that kind of world community tomorrow. Clearly, students must literally become citizens of the world. It seems obvious that they must learn a great deal more about their neighbouring countries than they know at present. We should expect in the ordinary citizen an awareness of the geography of his or her region, some knowledge about its various histories, an appreciation of the politics of the region, some understanding of its different languages and culture.

Knowing what we know about the shift from industrialism, these children in our schools must develop different kinds of skills before the nation in which they live can achieve these transformations in its earning capacity. They will need to have a far greater degree of sophistication about politics and political systems, about the economy, about financial affairs, about the way wealth is created and maintained, about the system of law and about forms of government. Every citizen will need to have acquired a core of common knowledge about these matters.

And they will have to be truly international. It is no longer tenable, for example, for Canadians to compare themselves only with other Canadians, in terms of education or employment or living standards or work habits or social life. For example, we have become familiar with the practice of providing certificates at the end of secondary education which purport to rank a student against the performance of those in his or her own age group in the same school-year in that state, province or country. But increasingly, what is taught and learnt by the same age-grade cohort in Japan, Singapore, New Zealand, Brazil, or Fiji is of relevance to all students. Increasingly, they will be competing for the same jobs, or trading against each other in a rival firm, or working as colleagues in the same enterprise, or mixing together socially in the global village.

We know also what a country, particularly developed nations, must do if the workforce is to be made competitive with its trading partners. If the services, information, and technological sectors of the economy are to be expanded to provide employment openings for a greater percentage of the workforce, then the 'educational water table' of the entire population has to be raised. As was pointed out in chapter 2, the tertiary and quaternary sectors have always tended to require not only post-school training, but usually also some kind of credential as a passport to practise.

Those who drop out of education or training will continue to cause enormous concern to society, not only because they will be at risk over finding employment, but also because they will not have the educational foundation on which to build new careers in the future. If students across the whole range of abilities are to be kept in school, then we already know that they will not be served well if they are force-fed a traditional, subjects-based, academically oriented curriculum created in the first place for that minority of the student population who hoped to proceed to a university or into the professions – and it is not at all certain that it was particularly good even for them. Over recent decades and in several countries, schools have developed a promising set of alternative programmes for students with other aspirations and backgrounds, and many of these programmes have given new hope to groups who were disadvantaged under traditional programmes.

If making the appropriate changes to schooling were a simple task, teachers and school administrators would already have accomplished it. Educators are great activists. They do not need structural or legislative reforms to transform their curricula; they do it every day as they prepare their lessons and their learning programmes. But this exercise is so large and complex that it needs more than teachers to get the task done. And it is not helped when the solutions invented by those not closely associated with schools are simplistic, naive, and will bring the very outcomes which society hopes to circumvent. Most importantly, the new programmes must be compatible with the new paradigm about the world.

It should now be clear that if the educational task were simply one of planning and implementation so that these changes were coherently built into the fabric of schools, the task would be awesome enough. Yet education for the twenty-first century needs something far more fundamental than all that. It needs those reforms, certainly, but it requires something more as well, and it is this 'something more' which has been so hard to define. If it is a restructure we are seeking, then it is one that affects our way of viewing the world. In short, we do not simply need a new package of programmes. We need a new spirit and a new outlook. The future of the world and that of its children depend quite literally on how well we can accommodate new ways of seeing in schools.

THE POST-BUREAUCRATIC ORGANISATION

The changes discussed above all point to the fact that, if education is to become consistent with the ideas outlined in the previous three chapters, it needs to be positioned in a new kind of organisational structure which is both post-bureaucratic and post-industrial. As has happened so often in the past, education is already being forced to adopt the modes of organisation which appear to be successful in the business or private sector. Bureaucracy grew out of an economy which was predominantly industrial, but the post-industrial economy is now spawning new forms of organisation. Put bluntly, a business which operates on bureaucratic lines cannot compete in a post-industrial economy which guarantees survival only to those firms which are flexible, which can make quick, strategic decisions, which encourage innovation and entrepreneurship, which value creativity rather than conformity, which give their members the power to take local decisions and to exercise initiative, and which regard the people in the organisation more as partners than property.

These qualities can be found even in those post-industrial organisations which appear to be huge, international, and multi-faceted. They have discovered that there are available models of organisation which are better than bureaucracy. The centre does not necessarily know best. While there are some frameworks, probably centrally devised, which all will honour, and while there is a set of priorities which all members of the firm must observe, it would be presumptuous, if not arrogant, of those at headquarters to think they should or even could impose controls on all the day-to-day operations of the firm, or monitor all the activities of its several parts, or make all the strategic decisions for all the company's members. Education systems and individual schools are now adopting the fluid, entrepreneurial, organisational patterns which characterise the new growth areas of the economy. If that is the case, then educators need to be clear what the post-industrial organisation looks like.

Charles Handy (1985: 389–412) has pointed out that some of the assumptions which we took for granted in the bureaucratic organisation are no longer believed. They no longer ought to be operative in education. They include the following:

- Specialisation is no longer seen as a strength. There is increasing emphasis on generalist (rather than specialist) skills;

the new organisation requires adaptable people who can turn their hands to several tasks and who view the organisational and professional world more globally than the narrow specialist.

- Hierarchy and status can be disabilities, particularly when teamwork and shared skills are needed. Collegiality, not hierarchy, now is favoured.
- And so is co-ownership. Every worker has a stake either literally or metaphorically in the company. The company does not belong only to those who put up the money in the first place.
- Staff are not property. The company does not own them. The company must not presume to be able to buy and sell them. Every person who joins the company owns part of it, and invests some of himself or herself in it. In short, the staff are stakeholders rather than employees.
- Salaries are out. Whereas a wage used to signify that a person is paid for the time he or she gives to the company, the new mode is that you are paid for doing a job, for rendering a service. So a 'fee for service' replaces being paid just for turning up at 9 o'clock. Contracts are replacing salaries.
- Equipment and machinery are not simply capital, things owned by the company. Rather, they are the means whereby the capacity of the people who work in the firm is extended; in short, they are tools. This distinction has been heightened by the advent of information technology which has enabled firms to shed many of the positions once occupied by middle management.

The constellation or network organisation

The kind of organisation which emerges has been variously described as a constellation, as a federation, as atomised, as dispersed, as a 'membership organisation', as a network organisation or as the 'shamrock organisation' (Handy, 1978: ch. 9; 1989, chs. 4–6). It is described well by Toffler in his book *The Adaptive Corporation* (1985), which analysed how the giant American firm AT&T should restructure to ensure productivity. There develops in the adaptive corporation a centre or core which retains 'tight control over technical quality, research and development, major investment decisions, planning, training, and coordinative activities' and which becomes 'the intelligence centre of a large constellation of companies and organisations' (Toffler, 1985: 129)

Toffler proposes a much more extensive shedding of functions to subsidiaries. He argues that functions which are repetitive (like cleaning), capital intensive (which require the purchase of expensive machinery or equipment), controversial (like media relations, counselling or social welfare) or which can 'piggy-back on someone else's capability' (like the production of some curriculum materials, evaluation, assessment, or research and development projects) could well be discharged by 'spinning off subsidiaries and contracting out' (ibid: 139).

By this means he developed an organisational structure which he called a constellation. At head office there is a relatively small, lean staff, a core which retains tight control over technical quality, research and development, major investment decisions, planning, training, and coordinating activities and which becomes 'the intelligence centre of a large constellation of companies and organisations'. Indeed, the corporation needs to employ only a core staff, smaller in number, more highly qualified, and more synoptic in its roles than the management staff used to be, a group 'whose essential product is leadership' (ibid: 128).

The rest of the firm's activities can be conceived of as separable, free-standing functions, the specialised operations which were once handled in branches and divisions. But these functions can be modularised, and then contracted or franchised out to satellite units or subsidiary firms who supply services or components to the mother company, and usually for a negotiated fee. As Toffler points out, it is not necessary for the modular operations to be performed by the firm, nor is it necessary for the firm to own all the subsidiaries which handle the modules. Some of them can be mini-firms, some operating as 'firms within the firm', and others as independent entities. Provided the service is carried out to the satisfaction of the parent company, the head office does not need to concern itself with the internal workings of the subsidiary nor to dabble in its work methods, or even to own it. Indeed, some of the company's best executives may be encouraged to form 'spin-off companies' with venture capital from the parent company and a contract to provide a guaranteed service for a price.

It is possible to list the characteristics of the network organisation, the post-industrial organisational format which is beginning to replace conventional bureaucracy, and the kind of organisational arrangement which would be more suitable for schools of the twenty-first century (Beare, 1990a). The network organisation:

- Consists of relatively small units within a bigger 'corporation'.
- The units are loosely coupled. What goes on inside each unit does not necessarily affect the whole corporation.
- The corporation is co-ordinated in a more or less organic, rather than a mechanical, way.
- The flow of information within the firm and among its member parts and mini-firms is not dominated by hierarchy.
- Organisational 'structuring' means designing the linkages among the activities performed by the units.
- The units do not need to be controlled in a hierarchical way, either internally or within the system. They are in fact collegially ordered. The units also relate to the core staff in a collegial way. The firm is much more egalitarian than the bureaucracy could ever be.
- The units are mutually dependent.
- Unit managers therefore tend to carry the full range of managerial tasks which once belonged only to the head office.
- It falls to the unit manager to mediate the demands emerging from his or her staff, from peers in the other units, the parent company, and the unit's clients. The unit manager has therefore been described as the man in the middle, an information broker, a negotiator and facilitator.
- The units operate on a provision-of-service basis rather than on a central-control basis. 'A climate of commands' is replaced by 'a climate of prohibitions'.
- All senior managers have a responsibility to promote or to preserve the culture of the firm.
- The units are expected to be pro-active, anticipating rather than reacting to events.
- The corporation is an 'ecology', an environment for inter-related activities.
- Networks and grapevines (that is, informal channels) are legitimate means of conveying information and must be managed by a unit leader. The 'paper warfare' is less intense than in a bureaucracy where files and paper records are essential to preserve the corporate memory.
- The internal dynamics of each unit are created by the unit itself. Providing it delivers its service efficiently, who but the members of the unit care about its internal organisation?
- The unit manager must operate collegially in the whole corporation, and must not adopt a 'top-down' or 'boss' mentality.

Out of this organisation comes a new kind of administrator:

> The new manager . . . will not be a classical, hierarchically
> oriented bureaucrat but a customized version of Indiana Jones:
> proactive, entrepreneurial, communicating in various lan-
> guages, able to inspire, motivate and persuade subordinates,
> superiors, colleagues and outside constituents.
>
> (Gerding and Serenhuijsen, 1987: 127)

These basic premises are now developing in educational organisations. The first major proposition stemming from the new
paradigm as outlined in the previous chapters is that schools must
begin to operate in a mode consistent with the future rather than
with the past.

ON PARADIGMS, SYMBOLS AND MYTHMAKING

In order to plan an appropriate educational response to the case
we have made about the new paradigm for education, it is
necessary to understand how we create these frames of reference
for ourselves, these new 'ways of knowing'. Developing in students
a comprehension of this process of building frames of reference
into our lives is one of the most important functions of education.

Observe at the outset that these transformations to the way we
view life are usually effected by means of *language*, by using the
same words, by consistent vocabulary, by repeated imagery. That is
always how we show the set of our minds. Language reveals our
recurring themes, our favoured ways of interpreting the world. In
order to cope with the complexities of the external world and of
our inward selves, we invariably choose metaphors and analogies
to systematise our vision, likening the unknown to the known, and
we use the formula over and over again. So our language tends to
repeat certain ways of seeing, and thereby it both constructs and
confirms our values and our belief systems.

Others then begin to 'read' us in the same way. Once our
favoured way of viewing the world becomes manifest, then others
can predict our behaviour with a fair degree of accuracy. We
become consistently understood. Unfortunately, we can also
become classified and labelled, imprisoned by ourselves and by
others in our own definitions. Scholars are only now beginning to
explore the powerful conforming behaviours which derive from
those stereotyped visions about what we conceive reality to be. As

Broms and Gahmberg (1983: 482) put it, 'The study of symbolism is now a new wave in organisational research'. That self-manufactured set of simplifications which we use to interpret the complex stream of impressions impinging on our consciousness is called a paradigm.

As noted above, the word 'paradigm' was made popular by Thomas Kuhn in *The Structure of Scientific Revolutions* (1962). It refers to a shared set of assumptions about how reality is construed; it emerges from our ponderings and thinking, from our beliefs and visions of self. In short, it grows out of contemplation. But paradigms are reinforced by constant revisiting of those things, events, memories, and people which we invest with folkloric qualities. For example, we create icons – trophies or memorabilia or semi-sacred objects which in some way embody what we take very seriously. We develop ceremonies and rituals, collective and recurrent actions or behaviours. And we develop shared stories, many of which become sagas, involving our own culture heroes. There comes a stage when all these things constitute the framework within which we plan, explain, conceptualise, act; the framework energises our concerns. By these means we build our cultural edifice, our framework of meanings. Schools can and should do all of these things.

One of the prime functions of education involves developing these meanings about ourselves as individuals and as a community, constructing our own authentic myths, legends, and belief systems, and building our understandings about social processes like education. It has been labelled the symbolic or the mythic dimension, and we all engage in it. As Chetwynd (1982: viii–ix) says, 'Everybody's waking life is full of symbolism.' This is the field in which educators work, knowingly or unknowingly. In addition, if we understand how paradigms are built, we may be in a better position to redesign our existing world-views. To help that process, we make five observations.

First, the paradigms or systems of symbols which shape our existence usually tend to start with real and even ordinary things or events which, when pondered and reflected upon, begin to body forth larger, deeper significances. 'Supernatural' is the word which was originally intended to convey this meaning; literally it signifies that which stands above and beyond the natural or the ordinary, beyond the facade we call the real event.

So the landing of Australian soldiers at Anzac Cove in 1915 is no longer just another skirmish in a war, but rather a symbol of Australia's struggle to be recognised as a nation in its own right. Again, the landing of a British Airways flight at Heathrow Airport may be a routine event of no symbolical significance, whereas man's first landing on the surface of the moon is an event worth celebrating. Or again, that same British Airways flight may be routine for an executive returning home from a regular visit to an Asian office, but it may indeed be the symbol of a new life to a refugee on board the same flight and arriving in an adopted land for the first time. For her it can be a kind of Passover event, its anniversary to be celebrated year after year. Those who can discern the significant and who can build symbols out of the fabric of their own and others' lives are apprehending life deeply, and are in the process of becoming significant human beings. Teachers ought to be like that, but they need some poetry in their souls to be so.

Second, symbol-making, myth-making, paradigm-building is the lens whereby we identify the deep things in our world. In his introduction to A *Dictionary of Symbols* Chetwynd (1982: xi) explains that 'symbols are concerned with what is of greatest importance to man, his own life and his own mind, the central focal point of that life'. And Weick (1976) has pointed out that our paradigms, our ways of seeing, also limit what we see. Many important things go unnoticed if our paradigm does not focus them. The guiding principle, he says, is a reversal of the common assertion 'I'll believe it when I see it' and presumes an epistomology that asserts 'I'll see it when I believe it.' (Weick, 1976, 2,3).

We see significances because of our belief system. Every person and every society has symbols which do that. Every school does.

Third, it was Campbell, the author of that monumental work *Masks of God*, who demonstrated that the mythic is far more fundamental to the development of the human race than economic or instrumental considerations. Every race and every age, from the dawn of civilisation to the present day, has invented symbols, stories, myths and legends, which put into picture and narrative form what lies too deep for technical explanations. Food, housing, money, and laws are, of course, important elements in the life of any person but they pale before the power of our belief systems. How else, Campbell asks, can we explain 'the economics of the Pyramids, the cathedrals of the Middle Ages, [and] Hindus starving to death with edible cattle strolling around them?'

This dimension transcends any instrumental factors, anything merely economic, because it engages people at the deepest parts of their being. Broms and Gahmberg (1983: 488) observe:

> The reason why myths are so powerful is that they are not only thought, they are also felt. . . . We cannot grasp the contents of similes, metaphors, and myths by rational reasoning. There seems to be something harder than facts behind these images.

Campbell put it this way:

> Mythology is no toy for children. Nor is it a matter of archaic, merely scholarly concern, of no moment for [people] of action. For its symbols touch and release the deepest centres of motivation, moving literate and illiterate alike, moving mobs, moving civilisations (quoted in Koprowski, 1983: 51).

Fourth, it is at this level that we transcend ourselves and become one with the mainstream of human history. In a quite astonishing way, the mythic tends to take similar shapes in all cultures; they are, Campbell says, 'themes of the imagination' with universal validity which, when bodied forth in rites, rituals, and ceremonies, become 'life-amplifying'. 'It would not be too much to say that myth is the secret opening through which the inexhaustible energies of the cosmos pour into human cultural manifestation' (Campbell, 1973: 3).

And fifth, many of humanity's prime discoveries and inventions in science and technology, the arts and civilisation, have been born as a result of myth and fantasy. It is as though myth gives human beings the imaginative reach to invade the realms of the incomprehensible.

> The human kingdom, beneath the floor of the comparatively neat little dwelling that we call our consciousness, goes down into unsuspected Aladdin caves. . . . [It is a] mythological realm that we carry within.
>
> (Campbell, 1973: 8)

What has mythmaking got to do with a programme budget, with performance indicators and outcome measures, with efficiency and economics, with industrialism and bureaucracy? A great deal, for to redefine education in an economic or instrumental way belittles one of the most magnificent aspects of all education, the aspect we have labelled the mythic. The question, then, is whether any new mythology about education is life-amplifying, whether it

substitutes the trivial for the profound, the banal for the transcendental, the cheap for what is culturally rich. A community
must beware lest it call the darkness light.

We are of course now standing on a plot of high ground looking
out across a new landscape which is vast and awesome, especially
for the educator. Several concerns arise from our contemplating
it, all related to the way schools form their particular culture, their
milieu for learning.

BUILDING A SCHOOL'S CULTURE

When we conceive of schooling, learning, the school itself, what
metaphors and analogies should we favour, which ones convey
adequate images, and how can we use these pictures to build a rich
school culture which acknowledges the mythic rather than the
mechanistic, the transcendent as well as the ordinary?

Conventional theories about organisations (including schools)
have been under vigorous assault for some time, though it seems
to have taken a study like that in Peters and Waterman's best-
selling book *In Search of Excellence* (1982) to make it abundantly
clear. Because 'corporate culture' has become a buzz term, it
carries the risk that we will pursue questions about group culture
in a way that is glib and superficial. We are dealing here with
depths and not surfaces, with the psychic and not the mechanistic.
In the school setting, educators are automatically engaged with the
power of symbols, of imagery, and of language.

As we pointed out in chapter 2, when large-scale organisations
and public schools began to develop during the Industrial Revolution, there were probably only two existing models upon
which to pattern the organisation of literally thousands of people
attached to a big institution, namely the army and the church – or
to be more precise, the medieval army, operating in the feudal
system before democracy, and the monastic, medieval church
before the Reformation. It should not surprise us that much of the
mythic in education has grown from military and monastic analogies, but it is useful here to consider how pervasively this mind-set
manifests itself within schooling.

We do not need to dwell on the similarity in organisation
between a school and an army. But the idea persists in other ways.
It partly explains, for example, the 'public school' infatuation with
contests of one kind or another. Not lightly was it said that the

Battle of Waterloo was won on the playing fields of Eton. Consider the way sports have been sponsored by the long established schools, and how the trophies of victory are hung in prominent places in the school. There are also rolls of honour for various causes. All this is redolent of the age of chivalry, of knights and feudal lords. It also persists in that continuing institutional device called Houses, derivatives from feudal times of the House of Lancaster or the House of York, small fiefdoms which exist to create a sense of competition or of tournament. Schools still retain emblems which include the devices of medieval heraldry like the ubiquitous shield, and they adopt behavioural codes like those imposed on the Knights Templar. School mottoes are often in Latin.

This paradigm about learning based on the age of chivalry has helped to create some of the most prized aspects of the culture of schooling. Indeed, we suspect that some long-established private schools are profoundly attractive to many parents because they have about them that atmosphere of chivalry, those heroic deeds of empire, and the virtues of medieval feudalism. That atmosphere encourages ceremony and pageantry, a sense of occasion, especially when the corporate body assembles. Of such stuff is culture, 'shared meanings', made. It should not surprise us also if an impression of competition, of winning against opposition, of grim battle and victory also pervades the academic programmes of schools.

In the same way, and especially because monasteries were the principal seats of learning throughout the Middle Ages, it would be remarkable if they had not left their imprint on the culture of education and on the way schools are organised. The system of novices (new-comers) who graduate through degrees or grades into more complicated study, acquiring ultimately the Doctor's (literally, teacher's) degree which allows them to speak authoritatively (as a 'professor', 'a speaker forth') is a pattern still retained in education. Indeed, so deeply is this progression through steps ingrained that it has proved almost impossible to break the curriculum for the academic elite away from the content-based, difficulty-graduated, traditional disciplines. The term 'discipline', of course, is derived from a Latin word for learner or pupil.

The monastic metaphor has also given schools some of their ennobling, poetic, values-oriented purposes. A school is often run as though it is a religious order or contemplative community devoted to teaching and learning, to personal growth, and to preparing the individual for service to and in the world. Not surprisingly, parents and the community have experienced difficulty in being accepted as anything more than peripheral in this process, for they represent the world outside the school, beyond the monastery wall, as it were.

It is also remarkable how many physical as well as symbolical features of the school conform with monastic imagery. The students are treated like novitiates ruled over by a Superior. In many countries they wear uniforms as the religious wear habits. The classrooms are configured like monastic cells; indeed school architecture and monasteries have strong similarities, including the long corridors, and a certain hushed atmosphere. There are systems of 'pastoral care' with each novice assigned to a kind of confessor. Frequently each building or wing is named after a saint, literally in the case of church schools, metaphorically in the case of state schools. The dominating physical landmark in so many schools, especially the older ones, is a tower of some kind, for all the world like a church steeple. The school property is surrounded by a fence or wall very similar to a convent wall, which allows the school to function like an educational retreat. The rituals and ceremonies of the school are often like traditional services of worship, including the singing of a school hymn and a ceremonial reading, or 'lecture'. Thus learning is conceived of as a kind of religious discipline, a training in a moral order, and aimed at building a certain outlook, including the willingness to serve in the outside world with altruism and honour.

Schooling as we know it is thus already paradigmatic, patterned heavily by analogies, metaphors and symbols, many of which are derived from a fairly distant past. Furthermore, the paradigm creates the tangible things about school – the way it is organised, the shape of its buildings, the nature of its ceremonies and rituals, the way the learning programme is conceived of, set out, and taught. Every school already has a culture, a consistent, powerful, conforming pattern for its members. It seems obvious that educators can unmake and remake those cultures, and usually simply by favouring a consistent way of depicting what they do.

Schools, for example, repeatedly play the 'language game'. There are quite different impressions conveyed about the school if the place where the chief educator works is called the Principal's Office, or the Head Master's room, or the 'Chief Executive's suite'.

Each title implies a different attitude towards the organisation and its members, a different vision about relationships, a different picture about that world of people. Every educator and every school daily spins a web of meanings which defines learning.

Every school (indeed, every organisation and every human group) uses rites and rituals too. They automatically grow up in connection with those 'difficult thresholds of transformation' where change occurs. Indeed we use the term 'rites of passage' and we typically observe them when a child is born, or is named, or begins formal schooling, at marriage, at death and burial. Many of these formalised acts of severance and reconstitution are part and parcel of education and learning. It is to be expected, then, that we will observe rituals over graduations, promotions, and certificates, and it is right to have celebrations at this time. These events are not merely organisational; they are symbolic, almost quasireligious. Many of the reasons why there are adverse reactions to restructuring school assessments, certification, or the shape of the school year, opposition to school amalgamations, to changing the names of schools or to altering the roles of teachers, stem from the fact that we are engaging here the supra-rational, symbolic, indeed the mythic dimensions of schooling.

Every culture also creates its own heroes and heroines. In the mythic tradition, the hero is the one who breaks through superficial obstacles to confront the deeper causes, there to battle the primal elements, and to win. By so doing, he or she demonstrates what we can all become; he or she symbolizes rebirthing, being made new. Campbell puts it in a beautifully evocative passage, using, appropriately, the story of the hero Theseus who slew the minotaur, the beast haunting the labyrinth of mankind's deeper being.

The heroes of all time have gone before us; the labyrinth is thoroughly known; we have only to follow the thread of the hero-path. And where we had thought to find an abomination, we shall find a god; where we had thought to slay another, we shall slay [our lesser self]; where we thought to travel outward, we shall come to the centre of our own existence; where we had thought to be alone, we shall be [at one] with all the world.

(Campbell, 1973: 25)

All great schools and universities have their heroes, people who embody the longed-for meanings and hoped-for achievements held dear by all the knights who have been initiated into the inner circle of that particular Round Table. Heroes and rituals derive from a reality contemplated by means of a shared perspective on the world. Schools create these mythic figures from among their students, from among their teaching staff or from significant others.

It is easy to find cases of how schools develop their own myths and ritual, and we here cite one. Wanniassa Hills Primary School was built into the side of a hill, literally, in a suburb south of Canberra. Its designers gave it a low-pitched roof in warm, earth-coloured tones so that it would harmonise with the landscape. The building itself is a symbol that this school belongs to the contours of its surroundings as its inhabitants belong to its community. The school is so discreetly positioned, in fact, and set below the brow of the valley ridge that you can drive past on the road above the playing fields and park area and not see the building.

In the opening weeks of its first year of operation, Wanniassa Hills school had awful teething problems. Tables and chairs did not arrive on time, the book deliveries were late, there was insufficient equipment, the builders had not completed their work; and so on. But the school's new principal had a sixth sense about community. He appealed for parent help, and it came. Mothers lent equipment; fathers volunteered to work in teams; furniture was borrowed; teachers and students cooperated with a disarming but untrumpeted forbearance that built goodwill. The school used its difficulties to construct a sense of community and common purpose.

In the euphoria of having overcome a common obstacle together, the extended family that the school had now become decided to celebrate its togetherness. So at the end of the first month of the school's existence, they planned a ceremonial and communal hike to the top of Mount Wanniassa, a modestly sized hill overlooking the suburb. Everyone went, mums and dads, little children and seniors, ancillary staff and teachers, and they picnicked together on the mountaintop. It became an annual ritual, a celebration repeated year after year to symbolize together-ness, to restate a sense of community, and to declare that this school is at the heart of the suburb called Wanniassa Hills. That school began to build the mythic dimensions of learning in its very first week of operation.

Every school can and does cultivate a world-view like that, by deliberately building images about who we are and how we relate to the world, teaching its members collectively how to go into the inner temple where myth, symbol and significance are made and loved. Every school needs to cultivate celebrations, repeatedly holding up that which is ennobling and life-amplifying. And every school needs to cultivate that concentrated, analytical, positive, passionate vision which enables each of its members to con- front the world with confidence. Schools are inevitably involved in myth-making. In short, then, educators can and do select the ways in which education and particular schools are described and developed. It is in their power to choose appropriate metaphors and to be symbol-makers for the next generation.

METAPHORS ABOUT SELF

The same process needs to be carried on in and for every indi- vidual. It is the school's responsibility to build and maintain in each child a constructive paradigm about himself or herself. There is now a large body of writing concerning how we create pictures of ourselves, how we define who we are and what our lives have become. Some of the images are plainly destructive, even affecting our mental and physical health. Others lift us to herculean heights of achievement and satisfaction. So any school which does not take seriously the creation of strong self-images in its students is simply an inferior school.

In a book entitled *Biography as Theology*, McClendon (1974) demonstrates how the images about ourselves which we carry around in our heads pattern the way we live out our lives. He cites the cases of Dag Hammarskjöld, the former Secretary-General of the United Nations who revealed himself in his posthumously published diary *Markings*, and Martin Luther King, the USA civil rights leader whose speeches and books are also self-revealing. McClendon wrote:

> Hammarskjöld understands himself as Christ's brother, as brother to the Brother; he sees the point of his life as a sacrifice to be offered; life is lived in the confidence that the unheard of is at the limits of reality. . . . King understands his work under the image of the Exodus; he is leading his people on a new crossing of the Red Sea; he is a Moses who goes to the moun- taintop, but who is not privileged to enter with his people into the promised land.
>
> (McClendon, 1974: 93)

We can find similar 'image-streams' (Fischer, 1983: 102) in other biographies – including those of Lord Mountbatten, Mother Teresa and General ('Blood and Guts') Patton.

Individually, too, we select our own culture-heroes, people whom we admire and upon whom we pattern our actions. To quote McClendon again (1974: 37):

> There appear from time to time singular or striking lives, the lives of persons who embody the convictions of the community, but in a new way; who share the vision of the community, but with a new scope or power; who exhibit the style of the community, but with significant differences.

In one way or another, we celebrate these people, returning again and again to their memory, to the story of their lives, to their achievements and vision. That person becomes part of our thinking patterns and of our celebrations, whatever form they take. Schools can foster the creation of heroes upon which to pattern one's life.

And again, schools can help students to create their own symbols and signs. When a person has a 'deep psychic or mystical experience', he or she has a need to establish some tangible memory of that event so that it can be celebrated. 'He builds a heap of stones (says Veilleux) or he builds an altar so as to live again the experience when he returns to that place' (quoted in Pannikar, 1982: 147). We can create monuments which are literal or metaphorical, institutional or personal.

It is Fischer's contention that Western civilisation is essentially afraid of dragons, of the mythic, and has not taught people to be at home with the world of metaphor, poetry, image and art, or to trust our powers of imaging; tradition, she says, is an accumulated series of stories which illuminate and fashion our fundamental meanings, derived from what she calls 'the prophet's gift of dynamic analogy' (Fischer, 1983: 153, 157, 159). The deepest perceptions about ourselves can often only be expressed in these ways. For that reason, education must engage and cultivate deliberately that depth, that mythic imperative, in each person. Schools can help every child to create paradigms and images of themselves, and of their world.

IMAGING, THE BASIS OF PARADIGMS

To ask people to step back from viewing the world naturalistically ('as it is') and to start viewing it reflexively as something constructed through experience, language codes, symbols, cultural signs, and so on is a difficult request, for it invites us to make relative what appears to be absolute, to make problematic what seems to be unproblematical, to admit that there may be no fulcrum, no foundation and no ultimate certainty. Yet a lot hangs on the proposition.

The belief that words simply 'mean what they say' and that texts and discourses passively reflect a 'real' world is a deeply held and comforting one, yet it glosses over the ideological uses of language and the many ways in which language mediates experience. To begin to engage in a more dynamic and open process does involve giving up a certain degree of comfort and certainty, yet what is gained in return is very substantial – greater freedom from ideological and linguistic traps, breadth of vision, the ability to 'speak one's own word', and direct access to fundamental negotiations of meaning (Slaughter, 1988). People who know that they are not simply in the position of passively decoding someone else's finished structures of meaning, but are actively interpreting and negotiating them for themselves can feel empowered because they are real participants in the process of cultural reconstruction and renewal. If they are free to reinterpret texts, it is just a short step to reinterpreting inherited traditions and normative views of desirable futures.

In recent years many devices have been developed to help in this educational task, self-reflexive methodologies which include interdisciplinarity, general systems theory, deep ecology and some forms of textual analysis (Devall and Sessions, 1985; Belsey, 1980). In short, there exist for individuals and for teachers simple techniques for engaging in 'negotiations of meaning', ways of dealing with students' fears, and workshop methods for 'inventing liveable futures' (see Gough, 1985, 1990; Slaughter, 1987c, 1991a). Such methodologies and approaches support views of the world in which we recognise our embeddedness in a series of contexts. We begin to see that our understanding of reality is dependent upon the quality of the models we use. Problem solving is no longer about making small, isolated changes, but involves participation and intervention in mutually interacting webs and processes. In this sense, the solutions are judged not by whether they are 'right', but by the degree to which they are elegant and stimulating. As Fisher notes, 'the contexts of elegance are dependent upon the illumination that enables us to see them' (Fisher, 1987:11).

Return for a moment to Lovelock and his comment that life is colligative. It is an unusual word; the rare English verb 'colligate' meaning 'to bind together' is derived from the Latin *ligare*, 'to bind', (which gives us the English word 'ligature'). It calls to mind that other word, 'religion', which comes from a similar Latin root. It gives an accurate description of what we all do. We are forever synthesising our views about ourselves, about others, about the cosmos, about reality. We repeat and repeat those views until we believe what we are telling ourselves. We bind to ourselves a patterned way of seeing or perceiving, and then we interpret our world out of that framework.

That is indeed why many people reject formalised or conventional religion. Because it does not line up with reality as they experience it, they jettison what does not look genuine, what does not render adequate explanation or prediction. The very act of throwing beliefs away indicates that a person has a robust and living religious view. For religion is that which we have bound to ourselves again and again; it is the frame, the casement, through which we look out on our world; it is our favoured way of seeing. It integrates the meanings we read into what we experience.

Of course, that way of seeing can sometimes be negative, destructive, even diabolical. It can literally destroy a person, or others or a part of the world. If, for example, one country constantly represents to its own citizens and to others that another country is a threat or is unfriendly, that belief can lead to an arms race which is called, rather oddly, 'security'. This point has been made cogently by Willis Harman in *Global Mind Change*. On the other hand, for some people their wholeness of seeing, their visioning, can lead to the most sublime acts of love, to the most breathtaking creativity, to the most awesome reaches of the human spirit.

Systems of beliefs, the fundamental assumptions on which we base actions, thinking, and living, once they are firmly held, start to manifest themselves in tangible ways, indeed as tangible things and events. Beliefs are self-fulfilling prophecies, for in a thousand incidental ways, by acting in one way rather than in another, by going to one place rather than to another, by giving priority in our thoughts and in our actions to one rather than to another, by choosing things, by talking about things, we create the conditions which bring into existence the very things we believe in! It is a widely demonstrated law about human behaviour that what you are convinced about manifests; it clothes itself in reality.

It is sad that we so often attach our beliefs and convictions to the wrong things, and in so doing we create the conditions to make them happen! Andersen (1954: 165) has written:

> We are so ready to see on all sides a hostile and preying world that we are constantly going about our daily tasks affirming our faith in disease, disaster, poverty, failure, and loneliness. . . . 'As ye believe, so it shall be unto you'. We shall have our beliefs anyway, why not make them beliefs in good, . . . in abundance, in health, in vigor, in integrity?. . . It seems strange most of us find it so much easier to attach our beliefs to negative things rather than positive.

We also allow our convictions to be shaped by others, by, for example, the arbitrary judgements of politicians, by what the newspaper editors select as their lead stories for the day, by the TV items which, after all, are selected from among literally hundreds of options available to them. We let other people control the agenda of our conversations. Our view about reality, about what is and is not important, we permit to be manipulated by someone else's faith or belief system.

Especially for young people, then, we must teach them not to give in so easily. *You* make the choice of what will dominate your life. *You* select the things which will fill your thoughts. It is a choice with awesome consequences, because the things which you allow yourself to become convinced about will come into being! There is a deadly seriousness, then, in those celebrated words of St Paul's as translated in the Authorised Version of the Bible:

> Whatsoever things are true, whatsoever things are honest, whatsoever things are just, whatsoever things are pure, whatsoever things are lovely, whatsoever things are of good report; if there be any virtue, and if there be any praise, think on these things.
>
> (Phil. 4: 8)

These are the qualities which fill a healthy mind.

Meanings, therefore, are never closed and 'finished', but 'open' and negotiable. There is never a final interpretation because we never reach a final perception. Meaning is derived from an active process of involvement and participation, drawn out, created, constructed by the work of focusing, attending and signifying. People have the power to re-create their world by renegotiating their perceptions and meanings. David Bohm shows in part how this process works. His account of the 'implicate order' suggests that the whole is enfolded in any part and accessible through it. Moreover, 'meanings are . . . capable of being organised into ever more subtle and comprehensive over-all structures that imply, contain and enfold each other in ways that are capable of infinite extension' (Bohm 1985: 75). At this level of integration new qualities emerge. As Bohm notes, 'if you go to the infinite depths of matter, we may reach very close to what you reach in the depths of mind' (Bohm, 1985: 90). This deeper awareness, as an instrument of knowing, may literally create new realities. It is this, rather than new tools or technologies *per se*, which leads on to new human and cultural possibilities.

Ideas like these are of immense value in serving to counterbalance the usual preoccupation with economics or technical evolution and development. They represent a significant departure from the stale conventionalism of much educational thinking and can begin to inform necessary shifts in theory and practice. Enough is known already to make the shift away from standard subjects and stereotyped forms of teaching and learning towards experiential, reflexive and meta-level frameworks of meaning. Neville has treated these aspects of learning in his *Educating Psyche* (1989), and Grumet has shown how the use of one of the self-reflexive methodologies, writing autobiography, can create new avenues for critical awareness (Grumet, 1981). We take up this matter of techniques and strategies in the next two chapters.

TOWARDS NEW REALMS OF MEANING

It seems ironical that constricting, imprisoning, small-minded paradigms are being imposed both on education and on the way we view our world just at the time when humankind is undergoing one of the most far-reaching transformations in its history, when expanded vision, liberated thinking, and a willingness to invent new frameworks have become essential.

Chapter 2 alluded to our passage from the industrial to the so-called post-industrial society, a change which is bringing social reconstruction on the same scale as occurred at the beginning of the Industrial Revolution. There are so many evidences at the present time of new boundaries being broken. Much of the pressure to go beyond the merely instrumental, to transcend the merely economic or rational, is coming, surprisingly enough, from some mathematicians and physical scientists. The great physicist Lord Rutherford expressed scientific materialism well when he told his students, 'All science is either physics or stamp collecting'. And the quantum physicist Dirac wrote, 'The main object of physical science is not the provision of pictures but the formulation of laws' (Woodcock and Davis, 1978: 12). But human beings carry around pictures inside their heads as a template to explain the world. Quite bluntly, stamp collecting may be more important – symbolically, metaphorically, mythologically – than Rutherford gave credit for. Thus we are witnessing a questioning of the very paradigm which gave the instrumental approach to education its legitimacy.

For example, the father of catastrophe theory, the French mathematician René Thom, argued in a paper delivered in 1979 that reasoning does not have to be mathematical only, the linear-logical kind so loved by universities, scientists and economists. That kind of reasoning is causal. It says, 'Because of this, then that; this follows logically from that'. But there is another kind of reasoning, Thom said, in which concepts are linked meta-phorically. It proceeds by saying, 'This *resembles* that; this looks like that'. He discovered catastrophe theory because it was 'a theory of analogy' (Woodcock and Davis, 1978: 160), developed from what Glassman (1973: 83) would describe as a study of isomorphisms.

Take another example. Freeman Dyson is a British nuclear physicist who worked with Oppenheimer at Princeton. In *Disturbing the Universe* (1981) in which, among other things, he speculates upon how to create human colonies in space, he makes the remarkable assertion:

> We shall not understand the dynamics of science and technology, just as we shall not understand the dynamics of political ideology, if we ignore the dominating influence of myths and symbols.
>
> (Dyson, 1981, 8)

He discusses the interplay of the economic and the spiritual (his words), concluding that human beings must now opt for 'living' technologies rather than for mechanical ones:

> In everything we undertake, we have a choice of two styles, which I call the gray and the green. The distinction between gray and green is not sharp . . . . The difference . . . is better explained by examples than by definition. Factories are gray, gardens are green. Physics is gray, biology is green. Plutonium is gray, horse manure is green. Self-producing machines are gray, trees and children are green. Human technology is gray, God's technology is green. Clones are gray, clades are green. Army field manuals are gray, poems are green.
>
> (Dyson, 1981: 227)

In the long run, he declares, 'green technology pushes us in the right direction' (ibid.: 234). For physicist though he is, he understands the universe as though it is a living entity.

> The more I examine the universe and study the details of its architecture, the more evidence I find that the universe in some sense must have known that we were coming.
>
> (ibid.: 250)

In essence, that is the same message in the book which has caused such controversy among scientists in Great Britain since 1981, Sheldrake's *A New Science of Life*. It is a direct attack on the reductionist-scientific method, which assumes that the universe behaves like a machine, explicable in terms of physics and chemistry, and governed by exact mathematical laws. Sheldrake explodes the paradigm by citing evidence accumulated (and not adequately explained) by the sciences themselves, concluding that the universe itself learns like a giantmind; we are parts of a living, growing, diversifying, learning universe.

One of the most dramatic expressions of this view about the changing cosmic paradigm is given by Capra, who is both a physicist and a student of Eastern philosophy. In his first book, *The Tao of Physics* (1975), he showed how remarkably similar are the statements about the nature of the cosmos being made by Western physicists and by traditional Eastern philosophers. The scientific paradigm which has ruled our thinking for several hundred years, he says, is in the process of being revised. We are at a turning point, a period of cultural transformation which will remake the way we view our cosmos. In fact we are manifesting the same symptoms noted at other historic turning points in mankind's development, before the fall of Rome and at the decline of the Egyptian dynasties, for example – symptoms like alienation, an increase in mental illness, violent crime, social disruption, and an increase in religious cultism. Capra declares:

> In the twentieth century, physics has gone through several conceptual revolutions that clearly reveal the limitations of the mechanistic world view and lead to an organic, ecological view of the world which shows great similarities to the views of mystics of all ages and traditions. The universe is no longer seen as a machine, made up of a multitude of separate objects, but appears as a harmonious indivisible whole, a network of dynamic relationships that include the human observer and his or her consciousness in an essential way. The fact that modern physics, the manifestation of an extreme specialisation of the *rational* mind, is now making contact with mysticism, the essence of religion and manifestation of an extreme specialisation of the *intuitive* mind, shows very beautifully the unity and complementary nature of the rational and intuitive modes of consciousness; of the yang and the yin.
>
> (Capra, 1972: 32; italics ours)

Capra's comment is consistent with the categories of Berman, discussed in chapter 4. It is a time of mind-expanding transformations, then, a time as perhaps never before in history when education and educators are free to explore new boundaries.

For of all the institutions which society has used over the years to guide cultural tranformation, only the school survives. The church once had the role, long before schools for all were conceived of; but the church no longer has the legitimacy, the centrality, or the popular acceptance to do it. The local community, in the shape of a self-contained village, was once a shaper of culture and identification; but the Industrial Revolution dissipated the influence of the village. Even the influence of family has been weakened by new patterns of childbearing, by working parents, by surrogate rearing, by new ways of making and dissolving marriages. Only the school remains as the one institution to which, at some stage of their lives, every member of society will belong for a sustained period of time. But the school has never been under greater pressure. A major rival is television, a means whereby every day of the year a consistent (even if predominantly crass) value system is promulgated to the whole of society. Other rivals for the attention of the young are popular music, computer games and sport. On the horizon we can see virtual reality and a whole new constellation of surrogate worlds rapidly approaching. With them come a range of new and challenging problems. Not least among the latter are the misdirections inherent in commercially motivated material concerning such major issues as technology, violence and futures (Slaughter: 1991 b). So the task of creating new realms of meaning, of building culture, of exploring the mythic and celebrating it, lies heavily on educators.

This chapter has discussed ways in which schools can be adapted to engage the new world-view. It has suggested some of the dimensions teachers need to be sensitive to, and especially language and organisational culture. So what can schools do? A great deal, even without changing their structures or processes very much. It may still seem an imposing task were it not for the huge, untapped potential inherent in the shift from past to future. To that topic we turn in the next chapter.

Chapter 6

The shift from past to future

The promise of technology lures us onward, and the pressure of competition makes stopping virtually impossible. As the technology race quickens, new developments sweep toward us faster, and a fatal mistake grows more likely. We need to strike a better balance between our foresight and our rate of advance. We cannot do much to slow the growth of technology, but we can speed the growth of foresight. And with better foresight, we will have a better chance to steer the technology race in safe directions.

K. Eric Drexler, *Engines of Creation*, 1986

By adding a future dimension to the learning process, we help to provide direction, purpose and greater meaning to whatever is being studied. By integrating past, present and future we act to strengthen a neglected link in the learning process.

Robert Fitch and Cordell Svengalis, *Futures Unlimited: Teaching About Worlds to Come*, 1979

Perhaps the single most important change of perspective that schools and teachers can make is the shift from a past-orientation to a futures-orientation. This has very many implications. In the old world-picture it was easy to ignore the fact that educational institutions were already heavily involved in futures. They did, and do, participate in a much wider enterprise – often without knowing it, without reflecting on the way that aspects of past cultures are brought into the present (literally, re-presented) and used as raw materials in the creation of futures.

No architect, engineer or business executive could proceed for long on the basis of worn-out designs and purposes. But as sheltered, monopolistic institutions schools are approaching the twenty-first century long before they have come to terms with the twentieth and, moreover, we have shown that they still retain many of the features of earlier times. This is not to attack schools, nor to take a crude anti-historical view, but rather to emphasise that the whole process of curriculum development, innovation and change has been bedevilled by the continuing immersion of educational institutions in the past – not the past that actually occurred in unrecorded complexity and richness, but the fragmented past that survives in reconstructed bits and pieces, replete with official myths, simplifications and omissions.

Schools, school systems, colleges and even universities have tended to behave as if the past were authoritative and the future a mere abstraction. Neither view bears scrutiny and competent historians will readily admit that their enterprise is much more provisional and open than is commonly believed. But few teachers, teacher educators or lecturers make a point of exploring the ways in which education inherently refers forward to ends and processes which absolutely *require* a future. When people ask us about 'what do we do' we are no longer surprised by the raised eyebrows, the incomprehension. 'Futures? What does that mean? What does it have to do with education?'

THREE COMMENTS ON THE SIGNIFICANCE OF FUTURES

Before considering the nature of futures work in schools, we offer three opening comments. First, wherever it lacks a futures dimension, education takes on a repressive character. That is, it elevates a concern for the maintenance of knowledge structures (and therefore power structures) over other human concerns. To render the future invisible, not worthy of discussion or study, is to strip away much of human significance in the *present*. For teaching and learning do not take place simply as a result of the pressure of the past. Statements of aims and objectives usually refer to purposes, goals and intentions which necessarily refer forward in time. So there is a contradiction in disregarding futures since they are already present, already there in present-day teaching and learning. Futures concerns are so deeply involved in creating the present that it is doubtful if we could act at all without them. Sir Karl Popper, scourge of historicism, put the point positively, and with emphasis:

the open future is, almost as a promise, as a temptation, as a lure, present; indeed *actively* present, at every moment. The old world picture that puts before us a mechanism operating with causes that are all in the past – the past kicking and driving us with kicks into the future – the past that is *gone* is no longer adequate to our indeterministic world. . . . It is not the kicks from the back, from the past, that *impel* us, but the attraction, the lure of the future and its attractive possibilities that *entice* us: this is what keeps life – and, indeed, the world – unfolding.

(Popper, 1988. Emphases in original.)

Like all other human activities educational work is embedded in time and it is axiomatic that such work cannot materially affect what has gone before. Whatever the precise purposes embodied in any particular educational offering they necessarily refer forward to future ends. While it is true that some activities are held to be worth doing for their own sake, and while it is earnestly to be hoped that good teaching and productive learning have immediate benefits, every lesson, exercise, tutorial, assignment and the like derive meaning both from what has gone before and what is hoped for in the longer term. Qualifications, the development of abilities and skills, vocational training and preparation for life are not short-term concerns. They extend beyond the here-and-now of immediate sensory perception to wider spans of space and time. They are true futures concerns.

Few teachers would undertake the rigours of training if it were not related to longer-term personal and professional goals. Students could not be persuaded to remain at their desks if they were not aware of some fairly powerful (but as-yet unrealised) reasons for doing so. It is not really possible to begin to discuss careers, personal development or social change without reference to the world of the future in which all of this is supposed to happen.

Second, education for whole persons needs a futures dimension. The implicit model of personhood which we have inherited from the industrial era overlooks this and much else besides. It recognises some of the mental and physical attributes of persons but deals scantily, if at all, with their emotional and spiritual aspects. By 'spiritual' we do not just mean 'religious.' There is plenty of religiosity around which does not adequately recognise the inner person and its higher needs. The latter has not been a part of recent Western culture in the past and it is therefore not seen as important now or in the future. Yet little can be more important (particularly for education) than to have a developed view of human growth and human potential which includes higher-order human capacities and motives such as peacefulness, caring (selfless love) and stewardship. This is part of the human basis for resisting technological overkill, and for reducing the role of greed, exploitation and short-term thinking. It is a major source of socio/cultural innovations which lead away from the abyss toward wholly different futures.

The industrial outlook needs replacing with a more comprehensive one – possibly one incorporating some of the characteristics discussed above. Such a model will give due attention to the layered quality of persons and the world in which they live, to the way in which we are all grounded in the physical world but also range upward through emotional and mental states to levels of functioning which can only be called spiritual (Schumacher, 1977). A world-view based on Cartesian logic and Newtonian paradigms of enquiry simply does not extend that far. But as we suggested above, the journey from lower to higher levels reveals emergent qualities. Just as a watch is more than the sum of its parts and a living cell is much more than the sum of its chemical constituents, so the highest levels of human consciousness do in fact reach the transcendent. A world-view or curriculum which misses this is actually missing one of the most humanly significant features of our world. For higher levels of awareness tend to be inclusive rather than exclusive. They reach out to embrace broad spans of space and time and have therefore become essential in healing our planet, creating peace and moving toward new stages of civilised life.

And third, as they are currently constituted, educational curricula tend not to offer a critical purchase on the underlying causes of the world *problematique*. They actually contribute to the problem when they unthinkingly reproduce an obsolete world-view. As we have endeavoured to show above, the sources of most world problems lie primarily in the paradigms and systems of valuation and thought which support the Western way of life (Berman, 1981 and 1990). The practical power of our technology and organisational ability has been purchased at an enormous price: pollution, conflict, alienation, social decay, ecological breakdown and long-term nuclear risk. Those features of the world are often glossed over, yet any map which omits areas of danger is not worth having. That is partly why we have argued that ways are needed of coming to grips with the underlying belief systems and approaches to knowledge which have brought our civilisation to this dangerous and unstable condition. While some may find this essential and constructive work threatening or even subversive (perhaps because of entrenched interests or dated knowledge) it cannot be overstressed that understanding the breakdown is an essential precursor to real cultural innovation and recovery. (We return to the notion of 'breakdown' in a discussion of the 'T-cycle' below.)

From the viewpoint advanced here, futures in education is most centrally concerned with negotiating and exploring new and re-newed understandings about our present cultural transition beyond the industrial era. It has a role to play in defining and creating a more just, peaceful and sustainable world. Visions and views of desirable futures always come before their realisation. Yet today positive visions are in very short supply.

To think ahead is still dismissed as being 'speculative' despite the fact that human civilisation has created dynamic processes of change which could alter, or eliminate, sentient life upon the earth. Such is the power of obsolete world-views. Empiricists will even ask how one can study something which 'does not exist'. But we regard the future (or futures) as principle of present action and present being. Without it there would be no plans, purposes, goals, intentions, meanings . . . or curricula. A present without any future component would be too sparse, too narrow, too arid for the exercise of human intentionality. Indeed, careful reflection will reveal that futures are constitutive of human consciousness. To the extent that futures are ignored, repressed or predetermined human agency itself is under threat. It is characteristic of our species that, while the body may be time-bound through biological necessity, the mind and imagination are not. In this view there is an organic quality to futures: they do not simply belong to experts. They are very much connected with everyday life and the wider implications thereof.

EDUCATION AND FUTURES

It is clear from the above that teaching and learning are activities which illustrate the interdependence of past and future. Without the past there would be no language, heritage or tradition to work from; without futures there would be no plans, purposes, goals or intentions to work towards. By its very nature, education is one of a number of social institutions which necessarily embrace aspects of both dimensions. But we have reached a point in our collective history at which the future requires greater attention than ever before.

When change was slow, technologies primitive and human populations small, the past provided reliable guidelines for the future. Today that is no longer the case. We are living through a series of multiple transformations, the final outcomes of which are unpredictable and unknowable. But the future is not an empty space and, contrary to popular belief, the study of futures is not more difficult or more problematic than the study of the past. It is somewhat different because the future has not happened yet. But that is precisely why it is worthy of attention.

The range of possible futures ahead of us is very wide indeed and choices are involved at every stage. It is possible that our growing concern for future generations has come too late. We may already have severed some essential link, some overlooked organism or process which is pivotal for all life on earth. We are certainly living right in the middle of a great global experiment to discover just how resilient the earth's life-support systems really are. But we are also witnessing rapid technical change and, for good or ill, new technologies always change the rules. What seemed impossible yesterday becomes commonplace today and forgotten tomorrow. So there are many plausible futures in which human life is transformed, extended, merged with machines, perhaps even transplanted to other worlds. Such possibilities should not be regarded simply as the province of science fiction writers and the entertainment industry. They need to be taken seriously by educators too, for they in particular stand at the threshold of past and future within the moving present.

The range of possible futures runs all the way from the inert radioactive desert to a vast solar civilisation beyond the 'high frontier'. The promise of the future is matched only by the threats of disaster, decline and exhaustion which are implicit in present ways of life. However, it is not the educator's role to campaign on behalf of a particular interest group or scenario. We need, rather, to attend to a more fundamental task: that of building perspectives about the future into everything we do. The rest of this chapter looks at some conceptual and organisational aspects of that task.

The next considers some practical implications, transitional strategies and resources.

FUTURES CONCEPTS

The most common deficiency in futures teaching is to 'look ahead' and simply extrapolate from the present. We call this 'the future of . . . ' approach. It means that aspects of our present world can become enlarged or exaggerated. Machines become faster, smaller or more dominant. Cities get more complex. People dress in futuristic clothing. Robots carry out menial tasks (and one wonders what people will do). This kind of optimistic, high-tech, business-as-usual future is, in our view, a kind of fantasy – albeit a widely-shared one. It is a result of extending our present as if it had more strength and durability than in fact it has. It misses the fact that there are indeed cracks in the foundations, aspects of our present world (and world-view) which are not sustainable. Extrapolative, business-as-usual scenarios tend to overvalue the role of technology and to underestimate human and cultural factors in the change process. They need to be be viewed with caution.

It is partly as a response to these problems that we emphasise the importance of futures concepts and methods. These are not used to forecast or predict 'what will happen' but rather to elaborate our understanding of futures in the present. Very many futures concepts are structurally simple, easy to use, and comprehensible. They can also be elaborated in depth. This means that when properly applied (that is, worked with at the appropriate levels over a period of time) they are capable of yielding much in the way of insight and understanding. Eight of these methods and concepts are mentioned here.

Rationales

The most important question to answer before attempting to teach about futures is 'Why bother?' Why ask anyone to think ahead when there are so many pressing demands in the here-and-now? There are many answers. Ten possible answers for education are given in Figure 6.1.

It is unfortunate that many misunderstandings about futures still serve to impede the wider application of the field. So, as a ground-clearing exercise, it is useful to deal with some of the

Rationales take various forms in various places. But among the most commonly cited suggestions are the following.

1 Rapid change means that many past assumptions, meanings and purposes are no longer valid and self-evident. In this context, past knowledge, and earlier modes and methods of representing knowledge do not command automatic support. Past experience becomes less and less reliable

2 Actions and decisions have consequences. In a world which is physically and socially interconnected, many consequences are displaced in space and time (for example, acid rain, ozone depletion and terrorism). Futures thinking therefore becomes a strategic imperative.

3 Foresight or careful forward thinking is preferable to 'crisis management'. It represents a saving of the energy which would otherwise be expended clearing up the mess.

4 Images of futures condition the present. Both positive and negative images feed back into the present and affect what people consider to be worth doing. These images are being continuously negotiated at all levels of society, though often in implicit, hidden ways (for example through advertising). Many images are ambiguous in that it is the human response to the image which is crucial, not the simple fact of the image itself.

5 Futures are not the abstractions they have sometimes been represented to be. Since they cannot be measured they have been illegitimately dismissed by an empiricist framework of enquiry. But the future (as a category) is a principle of present action. Without it we could not act at all. The human capacity to articulate plans, purposes, goals, intentions and meanings relies upon an open and undetermined future.

6 The taken-for-granted present does not indicate a specific period of time because the mental present has no firm boundaries. Aspects of past and future are enfolded within the present and schools can be much more explicit about what this involves for teaching and learning. Different time-frames can be matched with appropriate activities.

7 Education is a major institution which has strong roots in the past. Yet it cannot simply try to reproduce the past. It requires credible future alternatives in order to make sense of the present and to establish appropriate strategies and directions.

8 It is not possible to change the past, though the past is continuously re-interpreted (because we never stand at the end of history). Our relation to the future is different. We all exert our will and our intentionality upon it, and attempt to shape it according to our perceptions and needs. This is a much more active stance than we can adopt in relation to the past.

9 The implicit model of personhood we apply to schooling affects the way we view futures. If students are viewed as interpreters of culture and makers of meaning (agents) there is a direct connection between futures and the curriculum. This connection is obscured in more instrumental views.

10 Pupils are already alert to futures. Hence they do not need to be coerced into considering it further. They are naturally interested in the unfolding of their own lives. Many have fears about unemployment, pollution and nuclear war. It is important to help pupils channel the energies which support these fears into strategies which address the source of the fear.

Figure 6.1 Elements of a rationale for futures in education

possible objections. We have suggested that futures is not about making predictions. Prediction works well in relation to measurable systems and as an informal aspect of daily life, but it is impossible to predict the wider development of societies and cultures. Prediction in the latter sense involves a logical flaw. If it were possible, it would cancel out the all-important role of human beings as shapers and creators of history.

Again, and popular TV programmes to the contrary, futures is not about so-called 'intelligent' machines or creating a high-tech culture. We are not antagonistic to high technology; it is simply that the future (as a category) goes deeper than this. As a principle of present action and the forward-looking equivalent of history, it enables us to scan ahead, to exercise foresight and to act responsibly. To have *any* future worth living in will involve this basic shift of perception: a shift away from the past (which cannot be changed) toward the implementation of a range of futures-scanning and futures-creating processes.

The futures field

Futures work has often been misrepresented as being vague, abstract or just plain obscure. So it is important to provide some structure via two maps. One is a simple functional outline of the field, the other a conceptual matrix. Figure 6.2 provides a functional overview.

It shows three areas or foci.

Futures research

Here the emphasis is on forecasting, planning and exploring futures using analytic and quantitative methods. This area tends to be populated by specialists since some of the methods involved are sophisticated and costly. The money is provided by government departments and other large organisations, and the results of the work normally flow back to them. Hence very little futures research reaches the public – unless books are specifically written or digests of research results are produced.

Futures studies

Futures studies are located midway on the spectrum of futures

FUTURES RESEARCH (Major knowledge-seeking focus)	PREDICTION	Trend Extrapolation
	ECONOMIC AND TECHNICAL FORECASTING	Social Indicators Social Forecasting Technical Assessment
	SYSTEMS ANALYSIS	Global and Societal Modelling Long Cycle Research Simulation of Change Processes
	MANAGEMENT SCIENCE	Issues Management Decision and Risk/Benefit Analysis Policy Analysis
	SCENARIO WRITING	Ethnographic Futures Research Cross-Impact Analysis Delphic Surveys
FUTURE STUDIES (Synthesis, criticism and communication)	COMPARATIVE SURVEYS AND CRITIQUE OF FUTURES ISSUES	Digests, Indexes, Overviews of Problems and Dimensions of Change
	FUTURES IN EDUCATION	Professional Training and Development Curriculum Innovation and Course Development. Interdisciplinarity
	SPECULATIVE WRITING	Social Imaging Processes Creation and Falsification of Images Exploration of the Trans-rational
	NETWORKING	Global Communication Social Innovations Green Politics
FUTURES MOVEMENTS (Stimulating reconceptualising and possibly leading change)	THEORY AND PRACTICE OF ALTERNATIVE LIFESTYLES	Alternative Technology Reconstruction of Community New Age Cultures and Values
	HUMANISTIC AND TRANSPERSONAL PSYCHOLOGY	Futures Imaging Workshops Despair and Empowerment Work Psychodrama Psychosynthesis

Figure 6.2 The futures field: tools for managing change

work. This is where teachers, critics, writers and academics can be found. They normally try to balance specialised corporate work with the more informal approaches outlined below. This part of the field is therefore concerned with understanding the futures field as a whole, developing conceptual accounts of its work and communicating this to other constituencies and groups.

Futures movements

Many of those involved in such movements do not consider themselves 'futurists' at all, yet their activities do impact very strongly both upon the goals of the field and upon the society in which it is located. Social movements such as the women's movement, the peace movement and the environmental movement are closely associated with futures because, in their own particular ways, they promote broadly similar ends: that is, adaptation and change. They place new items on the agenda and create support for social innovations. The most successful movements contribute substantially to social change.

These three foci can in turn be opened out to reveal a very wide spectrum of activity indeed. The range illustrated here goes all the way from prediction at one pole to transpersonal psychology at the other. Does this mean that the field is just a collection of unrelated bits and pieces which bear no systematic relationship each to the other? We would suggest not. Some of the integrating aspects of the field are as follows.

- A shared conceptual and methodological base.
- Distinct theoretical perspectives and ideas.
- A clearly identifiable literature.
- A global network of organisations and practitioners.
- Regular conferences and meetings on futures themes.

All this suggests that, while the futures field draws widely on different modes of enquiry and merges into other areas at the margins, it does have a distinct core identity.

Another way to express this point is to consider some of the guiding propositions and assumptions which are commonly found in the field. They include the following:

- Under normal conditions there exists a wide variety of potential alternative futures.
- Such futures can be described as possible, probable or preferable; and these differences are important.
- However, alternatives are only latent until they are actualised by human action through such processes as participation, choice and responsible purposive action.
- The future is not predictable or predetermined; however, it can be influenced by the actions of individuals and groups.
- The present period has a number of parallels with earlier times

but is also different from them in important ways; choices made now will continue to exert their effects for many years to come.

- To exert some measure of conscious direction over the nature, pace, scope and direction of change is better than just letting things happen. The latter is risky and irresponsible; it merely increases the likelihood of high-cost social learning.
- In considering the world predicament, holistic, global and long-range perspectives are helpful.
- Images of futures condition present behaviour, and very many futures-related assumptions invisibly shape the way futures concerns are understood and expressed.

Such a list is suggestive rather than definitive, but it complements the structural outline given above.

A different way of considering the futures field is to regard it as a forward-looking matrix. Figure 6.3 suggests that futures work draws on a range of specific human capacities and perceptions. These utilize concepts and methodologies in order to study processes of continuity and change. The study of processes lends futures work an important empirical dimension, making it a good deal less woolly and speculative than has sometimes been suggested. Futures work makes it necessary to process a lot of information quickly. So those working in the field tend to skim, using the results of more detailed work carried out by specialists in other areas.

Figure 6.3 shows that futures work has diverse roots, yet it emerges as issues, themes and applications which are explicit and clearly identifiable. The applications may cover a broad area, but together they have clear social utility and many specific uses. It is worth looking more closely at some of these elements.

Futures concepts give expression to a range of innate human capacities such as foresight and vision. The interaction of concepts and capacities help to stimulate perceptions about futures. These perceptions (that is, fears, hopes, plans, purposes etc.) shape the progress of futures work and provide part of its subject matter. That is, hopes and fears for example can be studied in their own right, as well as providing a stimulus for other work.

Concepts, capacities and perceptions would not, on their own, be sufficient to allow futures enquiry to take place – except at a very superficial level. Methodologies are needed to increase the analytic and applied power of futures work, and to make it more

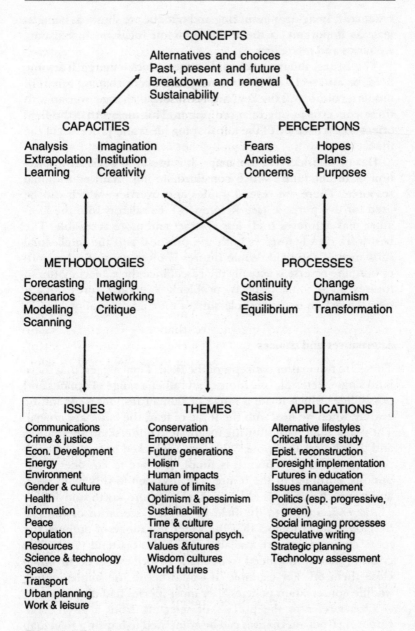

Figure 6.3 Futures study as a forward-looking matrix

systematic. Imaging, networking and critique are shown as being at least as important as the more common focus on forecasting, scenarios and modelling.

The issues, themes and applications which emerge from the field, or intersect with it, are among the major shaping forces of modern culture. All the key 'drivers' of social change overlap with these concerns at one or more points. This means that the field offers access to some of the key shaping ideas and processes of the time.

Having considered these maps, it is useful to consider a selection of the literature which constitute an important educational resource. There are several guides and overviews which can be used for this purpose (see References). Familiarity with the literature makes futures study less abstract and more accessible. The best work clearly displays both the practical and the intellectual substance of the field. While futures is often considered a 'soft' option, the reverse is actually the case. Since the subject matter of futures is, in some respects, problematic good futures work is necessarily founded on scholarship of the highest quality.

Alternatives and choices

These are two master concepts of the field. They suggest that there is no single, deterministic future, but rather a range of options and possibilities which invite a range of human responses. As will be evident when we deal with the topic of fear, the latter are crucial. The major reason for studying futures is to understand alternatives and the choices they pose. When we are locked in to a particular path or course of action, it is simply too late to consider other options. Fortunately, the future remains open in very many ways, and it is such openness which makes the future worth studying.

Alternatives refer to the field of possible scenarios or lines of development. It follows that the wider the range of options, the more choices there are available. Some choices tend to be 'time critical'; that is, they need to be made before events occur which close them off. For example, it would be no use implementing wildlife conservation policies after most species had died out.

Choices refer to the process of selecting from a given field. Choosing from alternatives can be compared to having a road map and deciding which route to take to a particular destination. The driving metaphor is also useful because it suggests that the view ahead may be more important than the view back. However, in general, the more time and effort invested in conceptualising alternatives, the richer are the available choices.

How can one identify what are the alternatives? They emerge from engaging with the subject matter over a period of time, from looking beyond the obvious, from examining assumptions and, perhaps, from using some of the major futures techniques like environmental scanning, the cross-impact matrix and the analysis of cycles of change (see Tydeman, 1987; Slaughter, 1988; and Slaughter, 1991a). In some cases, the major part of a project involves preparatory work of this kind. However, the result is a context in which choices have become progressively more visible. (This is certainly true of a major project such as the assessment of possible greenhouse effects.) A good deal of futures study and research exists to create exactly this, namely a credible, forward-looking, decision context in which choices can be made in full awareness of the implications.

Attitudes to futures

When the question of attitudes arises, people tend to think in terms of two polar opposites: optimism and pessimism. In general terms it is far better to adopt an optimistic attitude than a negative one. However, optimism and pessimism are polarities too simple to be applied uncritically to futures problems. The fact is that both terms are ambiguous. An optimistic person may believe that there is no cause for alarm when in fact there may be very good cause for it. Similarly, a pessimistic person may become so concerned about a particular problem that he or she will get up and do something about it. So the important thing is not a person's starting disposition but what, if anything, follows from it. The key to dealing with issues, concerns and fears about futures lies in dealing with the human response. We return to this in the next chapter.

One dominant attitude which is less ambiguous is the tendency to ignore the future, to devalue it, or to pretend that it does not exist. This unproductive attitude is captured in Sam Goldwyn's cynical question, 'What has posterity ever done for me?' Although such an attitude is quite startling, the fact that it remains common alerts us to a defect which is deeply embedded in the Western/industrial world-view. A different view is put forward by Kenneth Boulding who is quoted as saying, 'The future is the way I repay my debt to the past.' This indicates a more useful and constructive approach.

There is no doubt that, as a dimension of human experience, the future is more central, more 'present', than is commonly realised. So it is worth spending time exploring the linkages between past, present and future. Once we begin to see the tenses as artefacts of the language, we see more clearly our immersion in a universal process with no discernable beginning or end. These ideas are made clearer by considering the notion of an extended present.

Extending the present

How long is the present? A moment, a minute, an hour, a day? In daily life there are situations when it is essential to pay close attention to what is happening right now! Typing and driving are two examples of activities that require concentration within a fairly narrow time span. However, there are other situations which require reflection, suspension of judgement, careful preparation or forethought. There are indeed processes which our culture has created and which may extend over millennia. For example, plutonium is a lethal, man-made substance with a half-life of about 250,000 years. In this respect, our culture is already in the future.

So on the one hand we have a kind of 'default' notion of the present as a fleeting moment, the here-and-now, while on the other, and at a cultural level, we are looking at a span of 250,000 years. Clearly there are numerous choices to be made in thinking about the present. We tend to use different notions for different purposes, but without thinking about them very clearly. In other words, our choice of time-frames tends to be implicit and unacknowledged.

For the purpose of obtaining a grasp of our own context in time, our own particular span of history, we require a notion of the present which recognises that we are rooted in the past, responsible for creating our near-term futures, and also responsible for protecting future generations. In other words, by virtue of our deep connections both with past and future, we have a tangible need for an extended present.

The past has shaped us and the world we inhabit. We, in turn, add our own contributions to shaping the world to come. Some way is needed of recognising these relationships without overwhelming us. Elise Boulding has proposed an elegant solution; she suggests that we use the notion of a 200-year present; one that stretches a hundred years back and a hundred years forward. This time period has an organic quality because we are so richly connected to it through customs, institutions, values and, not least, through our families.We return to this concept in the following chapter.

Sustainability

If there is a single concept which challenges existing economic practice, and especially the notion of unconstrained economic growth, it is that of sustainability. What does it mean?

For something to be sustainable it must be able to continue in indefinite use without causing excessive disturbance or damage. In resource terms it implies continuous use without significant depletion. This definition makes immediate sense when it is applied to renewable resources such as fish or crops. Both can be harvested continuously because they are to some extent self-renewing. However, beyond critical limits, overuse may imperil the resource – clearly the case when oceans are over-fished or when soils are depleted by short-term exploitation.

A non-renewable resource such as petroleum cannot, by definition, be managed in a sustainable way. All that can be done is to reduce the rate of depletion, to expand the resource by exploiting lower-grade sources or to find substitutes. Hence the term 'sustainable' poses a very substantial challenge to economic orthodoxy. In effect, it calls the bluff of those who have forgotten that the earth (and its capacity both to yield up resources and to absorb waste) is finite and vulnerable.

But there is another important point. To look at the earth, with its rich geology, its vast array of flora and fauna, simply as a resource to be used is to adopt a particular set of assumptions and beliefs. First, they imply that people and nature are separate; second, that human beings have intrinsic rights to exploit natural systems for their own purposes; and third, that such use is not subject to any overriding limitations. Such assumptions have been taken for granted within industrialised cultures. Other cultures have conceived of person/nature relationships quite differently. Some have seen human beings as continuous with nature, both having shared qualities which make simple unidirectional use unwise, and sustained exploitation literally unthinkable.

So by asking 'Is this activity sustainable?' we are uncovering some underlying issues which were obscured during the boom years when the earth seemed limitless and invulnerable. The sustainability criterion asks us to reconsider our values, beliefs and practices. Some of the awkward questions to arise include the following:

- Are Western methods of farming sustainable? If not, why not and what could be done to make them so?
- How could our present use of petroleum be modified to reflect its true value and scarcity?
- What is a resource? Who decides, and how? How might a resource be reclassified (or even declassified, that is, removed from the resource category)?
- Would questions of sustainability be resolved if, instead of assuming a finite earth, we moved towards a space-based perspective by, for example, building solar power satellites and mining the moon?

Creating futures

The central point of teaching about futures is to show that we are all involved, all capable of pursuing ends and purposes which lead away from some outcomes and toward others. It helps individuals feel able to contribute to *ends which matter* and not to feel intimidated by the vast collectivities of power, prestige and profit which may sometimes seem overwhelming. (Some possible 'ends' are mentioned below.)

Futures are scanned routinely and informally by everyone. If this were not true, then we could not organise a holiday, let alone implement a curriculum or raise a child. Futures are scanned routinely and systematically by forecasters and strategic planners. Futures are created or avoided by the sum total of formal and informal processes by which important social decisions are made and acted upon. All these processes can be clarified, studied, subjected to careful and informed analysis. Moreover, individuals are free to participate in them. A careful and critical review of the work of citizen action movements shows that governments are often the last to know when a major shift is under way. Many such shifts developed, grew and gained legitimacy largely because people cared enough to get on with the necessary work.

Neither governments nor corporations are impervious to articulate public opinion and the latter can always be engaged by persons of good will who have something constructive to say. Hence, there is a notion of active and responsible citizenship at the centre of futures teaching.

Possible futures, preferable futures and global agendas

We have suggested that a very wide span of futures is possible. Those which are presently probable depend upon a reading of the current situation and of the prospects which spring from it. We do not here want to reiterate the many dimensions of the world *problematique* outlined above. Yet, it is clear that we have already moved too far too fast and without regard for the consequences. Hence, as a species we are now beginning to pick up the bill for earlier mistakes. We expect this process to intensify greatly. Humanity will learn both to deal more appropriately with past mistakes and to avoid some of the worst ones in future.

Such a commitment implies a global agenda. Many attempts have been made to define such an agenda, but each item on it must address four major factors:

- How to clear up the mess;
- How to make the shift toward sustainable economies;
- Deciding what we want to achieve with our innate capacities, with our technologies and with the earth;
- Exercising foresight.

The first factor for the agenda is already occurring through the voluntary work of many individuals and groups. As the links between our well-being and that of the environment become unavoidable, we can expect that clearing up the mess will eventually carry the force of a social imperative. This is as it should be. Whole communities may eventually spring up among ravaged landscapes, dedicated to ecological reconstruction and renewal.

The second factor is also gaining ground, but it poses much greater difficulty because there are so many profound contradictions embedded in social and economic systems which developed under quite different circumstances and assumptions. These contradictions concern such matters as economic growth, the nature of limits, person/nature relations and so on. They will take some time to resolve, and the resolutions will not be without conflict and hardship. But come they will because unsustainable economies are simply that.

The third factor also carries its own deep and challenging agenda. If we have been subjected to decades, possibly centuries, of misdirection about what constitutes 'the good life', about what is worth knowing, doing, and striving for, then just to be in a position to 'decide what we want' implies an enormous act of recovery. We are challenged to come to grips with the multiple breakdowns of the industrial culture and to reconstitute a culture on new or renewed lines. Since this is an historically unprecedented process, we cannot expect to have a detailed list of instructions. However, this does not mean we are helpless – there are very many constructive options which can be developed and explored. Some concern the foci we have already mentioned. Others go deeper and imply a kind of 'epistemological reconstruction' at the roots of our ways of knowing and being.

Finally, foresight needs to be used in all areas of education, planning and social policy. Fortunately we do not have to invent a new principle because, in some ways, we already understand the necessity of foresight. Traditional sayings such as 'look before you leap', 'forewarned is forearmed' and 'a stitch in time saves nine' clearly indicate that the principle is understood in personal and traditional contexts. We now need to extend it to deal with emergent concerns at the social level. This means creating purpose-built institutions and processes to inform our decision-making across the board.

If that sounds a bit abstract, consider three specific examples. First, climate change. It is well known that industrialisation has changed, and is changing, the chemical composition of the atmosphere. Should we just adopt a wait-and-see policy? If we did, we would almost certainly have to *experience* some devastating climatic changes before attempting to do something about them. Learning by disaster is a very poor and very expensive approach. Also, there are clearly lags involved in such complex systems. So it makes sense to monitor the situation, develop models of what could happen and use the results to continually update policy. Second, the human genome project which is now taking place aims to map the entire length of the human DNA sequence. It will probably be completed by early in the next century. But should we wait until then before considering the implications? Hardly! The students now in school and at college will live their lives in the context of the new moral and ethical dilemmas involved. We, and they, need to be informed about the issues before they become a scientific *fait accompli*. Third, nanotechnology appears to offer options for the fabrication of sophisticated materials and micromachines, opening up a staggering array of possibilities (Drexler, 1986). Some are so radical that they could undermine the material foundations of life. For example, replicating assemblers, as they have been called, may make it possible to grow machines in huge vats. (After all, this is how human beings, blue whales etc. are constructed. Nanotechnologists see themselves as 'improving on nature'.) If this turns out to be the case, they could usher in a manufacturing revolution, or they could be misused as offensive weapons. Again, the technology is so potentially powerful it needs to be controlled during its development. Once it exists it may be too late. Would the private car be in such wide use today if we had known more of its full costs? It is doubtful.

School curricula which embody some of these notions as central (rather than peripheral) concerns are literally facing in the right direction, raising common concerns which must be faced and resolved if succeeding generations are to secure their own futures.

THE ORIGINS OF FUTURES IN EDUCATION

Creating and sustaining curriculum changes and innovations is partly a matter of confidence. So it helps to know that this shift from past to future has been occurring for well over twenty years. The first school courses to deal explicitly with futures were taught in the USA and Canada in the mid 1960s. They drew upon the wider field of futures research. Techniques of planning, forecasting, war-gaming and scenario analysis were seen to have value well beyond their early strategic applications. With a number of other techniques they were steadily assimilated into business, industry, government and, finally, education.

Even today, when futures research and study are a global concern, the USA remains the heartland of futures work. It has more forecasters, consultants, futures researchers, marketing analysts and science fiction writers than any other country. So when the first school course was taught there in 1966 it was because people had already seen dramatic changes and knew that the future could no longer be simply assumed. Whereas once it had arisen fluidly and unproblematically from everyday events, now there were more and more possibilities, some of them not particularly desirable.

Educators began to incorporate futures elements into their teaching. They were assisted by pilot projects funded by the then Office of Education and these led to the establishment of centres where futures were studied and taught. The University of Houston in Clear Lake City still offers one of the most comprehensive Masters programmes in futures, but there are now many others around the world. The World Future Society entered the picture and by the early 1970s its education section had a professional membership of several thousand. Conferences, publications and seminars followed all over continental America and in other countries. By this time a number of international networks had sprung up, perhaps the most durable and productive being the World Futures Studies Federation.

In virtually every Western country, groups of innovators based in schools, colleges and universities began to communicate and to learn from each other. A perception grew that they were indeed part of a wider process, a movement away from immersion in a taken-for-granted present to a conscious evaluation of possible, probable and preferable futures. While the futures in education movement in the USA seemed to falter under increasingly unfavourable economic and political conditions, others took up the work which had been started there and improved upon it. Today on a global scale there are thousands of teachers, lecturers and researchers with interests in futures and education. A fairly recent initiative is the Prep 21 (Preparing for the twenty-first century) network which aims to survey and link those who teach futures in tertiary contexts around the world.

With a quarter of a century's experience to draw upon, it is quite clear that futures is not a bandwagon, not a 'flavour of the month' diversion. It may appear new in a particular context but it is certainly not untested in practice.

IMPLEMENTATION

There are basically three approaches to implementation.

- The introduction of discrete futures units and modules into an existing curriculum programme.
- The introduction of futures as a dimension of existing subjects and curriculum foci.

- The reconceptualisation of a school's *modus operandi* according to a futures paradigm.

The third approach is the most ambitious and it has not been tried in many places, although we discussed in the previous chapter some of the ways in which a school would change if it adopted the futures paradigm. Examples like the Montclair Futures School in New Jersey show that it is a viable option where resources, staffing and support are available. The approach does presuppose that training, materials and leadership are available locally, and this is clearly not always the case.

Approach Two requires that a 'prime mover' such as a head teacher or a curriculum coordinator take on the task of stage-managing a school-wide shift in content and process. Given the right environment, such a reconstruction represents a viable approach. When teachers are given the time to familiarize themselves with futures concepts and approaches, most tend to change what they do in small but significant ways. Since futures is a cross-curricular dimension, it can be approached this way. Schools and colleges are therefore increasingly using 'futures weeks' and professional development forums for this purpose.

The first approach remains the commonest since it means that highly motivated, individual teachers can innovate in their own classrooms without disturbing established practices elsewhere. It is becoming increasingly common for general studies, social and lifeskills, careers, domestic science, languages, drama and design (to take several examples) to include an explicit futures component and many new courses have been designed along these lines. Elective courses in futures *per se* will become more common as suitable course materials become available along with those willing to teach it.

GUIDELINES FOR SUPPORTING FUTURES IN EDUCATION

Futures in education began as a small-scale movement in one country, but, like foresight work in general, it has now outgrown that original context and become a structural necessity. It is becoming increasingly clear that an education based largely on what has happened in the past is unable to cope with the dangers and realities of the new millenium. So schools and school systems will need strategies for integrating futures into every aspect of their work. While the details will vary from place to place, it is prudent to observe a few general guidelines.

1 Futures work is at its strongest when it is grounded in the theory and practice of the parent field and of futures in education. It is important to draw fully on both areas in the creation of new courses, modules, training programmes and the like.
2 Perhaps the commonest error in teaching futures is to take a simple extrapolative approach ('the future of . . . ' approach). We have shown above why this approach is unhelpful. Because the field has so much more to offer, it is worth taking time to locate the kinds of critical methods and approaches which probe beneath the surface of change and reveal some of the underlying causes of world problems (and their possible solutions). This is partly why we have stressed the analysis of world-views.
3 It is helpful to relate local work to that done in other places. This makes it unnecesssary to reinvent the wheel. There are several organisations and publications listed below which can provide effective contact with others working in the same field.
4 Careful thought should be given to evaluation and quality control. These have been among the weakest aspects of futures in education, and they need to be incorporated in new programmes.
5 While there are still too few places where futures approaches are taught as part of initial, or in-service, training, there is a very considerable latent demand for such opportunities. The demand is largely unrealised because futures approaches are still not well understood – they have not been part of the traditional model of education. Yet the responses of people whom we have worked with over a number of years suggest very strongly that such approaches have a range of welcome consequences. These include:

a distinct increase in informed optimism;
an enhanced ability to move more easily between different fields and frameworks of enquiry;
a much clearer grasp of the world predicament and of possible resolutions to it;
an enhanced sense of purpose and mission in teaching and learning; and
an easy familiarity with the concepts and methods involved.

These outcomes seem to hold in general terms for students as well as teachers. The explanation is simple. Futures approaches provide tools of understanding and strategies for acting. They give people more control over their world and a greatly improved sense of purpose and direction.

6 Finally, there is clearly a need for longer-term innovation and support. Universities, colleges and state departments ought to provide this support. So long as they do not become ivory towers, remote from practice, tertiary institutions can provide greater depth, coherence, training and professional development.

Very occasionally a new insight or approach will illuminate the taken-for-granted world in a new way. This was true of the theory of evolution. It was true of quantum theory and of the view back of the planet Earth from space to which we alluded in chapter 3. In a more modest way the shift from past to future in education represents just such a pivotal change. The weaknesses inherent in some earlier approaches have largely been eliminated and a systematic approach to futures work can now be implemented. This means that schools can take up the available tools and integrate them into every aspect of their work.

Far from being a distant abstraction, the study of futures has now become indispensible within education, as elsewhere. We have devoted a whole chapter to this topic because, by drawing fully on the field, it is possible to open up quite new options for innovation and development in education. In this way and using these techniques, schools can participate fully in the transition process, properly fulfil their obligations to society at large, and produce a generation of younger citizens whose outlook is sufficiently robust and enlightened to ensure that the earth survives and prospers in the twenty-first century and beyond.

Chapter 7

What can I do? Some bridging strategies

Rates of change in these decades are such that people . . . are continually being taken by surprise by developments that should not have surprised them if they had a longer time perspective. . . . This fact of being continually taken by surprise is one of the major obstacles to imaging the future. If one is mentally out of breath all the time dealing with the present, there is no energy left for imaging the future . . . .

I propose as an answer . . . training in thinking in a time-span which I call the 'two-hundred year present'. It is not too long, not too short, and accustoms the user to the concept of continuously emerging orders. Its chief virtue is its organic quality. The two-hundred year present moment begins one hundred years ago today, on the day of the birth of those among us who are centenarians, celebrating their hundredth birthday today. The other boundary of this present moment is the hundredth birthday of the babies being born today. It is a continuously moving moment, always reaching out one hundred years in either direction from the day we are in. We are linked with both boundaries of this moment by the people among us whose lives began or will end at one of those boundaries, three and a half generations each way in time. It is our space, one that we can move around in directly in our lives, and indirectly by touching the lives of the linkage people, young and old, around us.

Elise Boulding, *The Dynamics of Imaging Futures*, 1978

Be confident about 'the future', then, and of your part in it. 'Ah, but what can I *do?*' you might legitimately ask. It should be clear from the earlier chapters that such confidence will be misplaced unless more robust ways of knowing are developed about the present and the future. There are many things we can do about that! For example, there are at hand many techniques and methods which help us to come to terms with what we feel, imagine, and believe – and they ought to be used in classrooms. They can also be used personally and anywhere else where people want to confront the future positively. This chapter deals with some practical strategies which can be employed to respond to the issues identified in the earlier chapters. We provide first some general guidelines for dealing with key issues and concerns. Next we suggest some specific teaching and learning strategies which might be used. We then show how these strategies can be applied at three levels: by the individual (including the teacher), by schools and by school systems. The strategies can of course be used in other contexts as well. Finally, we give answers to some of the more awkward questions asked about the processes.

THE PRACTICAL OBJECTIVES

The primary purpose in developing a forward-looking approach to education is to help people, especially young people, to build a genuine but qualified optimism about their ability to determine their own life prospects, and to give them the power to exercise some control over their destinies. Informed optimism grows from possessing at least three kinds of knowledge:

- an adequate understanding about one's own society and the world;
- an awareness of one's own vocation or sense of purpose; and
- knowing about skills of self-mastery and how to put them into practice.

People, including students, need to see themselves as agents and not as mere spectators and be given the chance to develop autonomy through decision-making and choice. In this respect there will be some structures which immediately get in the way and ought to be sidestepped, at least some of the time. For example, the knowledge structures which come to us in the form of stereo-typed subjects and disciplines (and schools are full of them!) can work against the development of optimism and empowerment because they confront the learner with pre-givens requiring accommodation and acceptance, not reconceptualisation and creativity.

With this confidence, and as insight develops, a learner can be encouraged to refuse to accept many of the artificial boundaries which our culture has read upon a seamless and indivisible world (Wilber, 1979). Two consequences follow. First, removing and reinterpreting boundaries eliminates the causes of many conflicts; in fact many of the conflicts tend to look foolish when we comprehend our common involvement with the same 'ground of being'. Second, removing artificial boundaries allows a person to explore his or her own immersion in wider processes involving issues of energy, food, relationships and meanings (Dossey, 1982). As the sense of inextricable involvement develops it provides the basis for a well-grounded stewardship ethic. This awareness of stewardship is now widely accepted as a crucial aspect of any liveable future.

A related attitude is the willingness to join with others both in defining and then in working to achieve shared goals and purposes. It is all too easy to drift passively toward protest. But beyond protest lies the essential task of defining in positive terms just what is wanted and needed.

Each person needs to develop images and concepts of his or her own goals for the future. This 'future-focused role image', as it has been called, is not just a piece of wishful thinking, or it need not be. The views people create for and of themselves deeply condition what they believe to be worth attempting in the here and now. Some of the curricula currently in use in schools obscure this important process, but the 'future-focus' can be made explicit, almost anywhere, through stories, time-lines, values clarification and many other futures exercises (Slaughter, 1988, 1991a). There are several kinds of skills which can be learnt to help in these processes. They include:

- self-knowledge; and empathy with others (the ability to get inside the consciousness of someone else);
- reflexivity (the ability to stand back from one's immersion in social processes and to reflect critically upon our debt to particular traditions and forms of knowledge);
- clarity about values, meanings and purposes;
- a broad or holistic understanding of global processes;
- the ability to understand and critique the images and plans of futures as they are represented (literally, 'brought into the present') by powerful groups;

- understanding the differences between possible, probable and preferable futures.

Such skills are developed as students work over a period of time with the ideas, resources and enabling processes which are available in this area. It is worth re-emphasising at this point that the study of futures does not aim to predict, not to say what *will* happen. That is the task of professional forecasters, and their work can certainly be used in education. The goal is not to make students into futurists but rather to help them understand what their options are. In so doing they can introduce into the present a wide range of choices – for example, in relation to energy, transport, lifestyles, and relationships.

Making an informed choice is what leads us towards one future and away from another. As was pointed out in the previous chapter, there exists a very wide range of possible futures. But while many things are possible, not all of them we would want to support. A few of the options are probable and it is here that one can draw on forecasts, projections, scenarios and stories to grasp the range of what is currently considered likely. Many of these options, it must be admitted, rise and fall according to how the media cover them, but that treatment is not a reliable guide to their importance. Preferable futures are those which we positively hope for and work to create.

Some of the criteria we can use in constructing our images of preferable futures are closely related to those commonalities of human experience which have been referred to above: sustainability, health, peace, justice and so on. The worries and fears which arise when these issues are confronted should be acknowledged, but they can then be focused and turned towards constructive and creative ends (see Macy, 1983).

TEACHING FOR THE 21ST CENTURY: SOME GUIDELINES

It should now be clear that we do not need new curriculum packages, or more courses of integrated studies, or to improve the traditional subject disciplines, for that would be to operate out of the old paradigm. Rather we need teaching and learning which are in the strictest sense of the word *moral.* We need to be aware that in a thousand small but cumulative ways, teachers, schools, classrooms and curricula impinge on a student's mores, and they are cumulative, built up step by step over time with consistent purpose. In short, the futures perspective is not an add-on, but something which interpenetrates the fabric of teaching and learning. It is a style of mind rather than another curriculum module.

Parents and teachers affect a child's outlook day by day and almost incidentally. Yet there are some fairly simple, deliberate things teachers and parents can do to build the balanced way of seeing which this generation needs for survival – personal, national, international and planetary. Let us briefly suggest ten.

First, watch your imagery. Choose your metaphors with care. By representing the universe as mechanical, something which works like a clock rather than like a living creature, we reduce a complex, fascinating, living world to a set of abstract formulae, driving higher qualities out of the cosmos, demythologising the world, destroying the wonder and the mysteries which produce poetry, music and art. Yet it is the physicists and mathematicians who have changed our perception about the universe by changing the metaphors they use. It behaves not like a machine, they tell us, but like a mind – learning, developing, becoming, in our very act of discovering it.

Second, teach for wholeness, for balance. The ancient view was that the world-order is an incredible balance of harmonies, represented by the Hebrew word *shalom* – the peace, balance, fulfilment, order, well-being which pervades the universe. That which produces disharmony or lack of balance, which diminishes the well-being of ourselves, or of any other creature on the planet is to be condemned, no matter by whom or what it is caused. Essentially, then, the disconnected, materialist approach to knowledge, to our planet, to the cosmos fails to show that we are all responsible for the whole. Creating discord, destruction and disease are evil acts. Can we be confident that their opposites – wonder, awe, reverence for our universe – infuse school curricula? They could.

Third, teach identification, connectedness, integration. Professor Arne Naess, a Norwegian scholar in the philosophy of science, in giving his Roby Memorial Lecture entitled 'An Ecological Approach to Being in the World' (1986), proposed that our individualisms endanger the world, and that it is necessary for us to identify with our cosmos in order to restore our collective health. 'There must be identification in order for there to be compassion,' he argued. 'Self-interest' has to be raised to a new level where we realise that we contribute to everyone's well-being by loving our environment. So, he asserts, 'the "everything hangs together" maxim of ecology applies to the self and its relation to other living beings . . . and the Earth. . . . Every living being is connected intimately'. We underestimate ourselves by being selfish, for we are 'much greater, deeper, [more] generous and capable of more dignity and joy' than we think. It ennobles us to act as part of the ecology of the universe (Naess, 1986).

It is significant that Naess uses the two words 'empathy' and 'compassion' to express a right relationship with the universe. 'Empathy' means getting inside the skin of the other and having the emotions and the perceptions that the other experiences. 'Compassion' has exactly the same original meaning, except that it comes from Latin and not Greek. It means to feel with, to have the same 'passion' as someone else. In both cases, the words invite us to enter into and be part of the consciousness of the Being, the livingness, which inhabits the universe.

Fourth, teach children not to accept blindly the value-sets other people try to foist on us. Let us put that in a practical way. If the television news disturbs us because it dwells on the latest murder, or on war, or on some scandal, it can be turned off. We do not have to accept the priorities being paraded before us. If the stories regularly appearing in the morning newspapers fill us with unease, foreboding or ill-will, we can simply decide not to read them, or at least not at that time. We have the choice to fill that first half hour instead with the ideas, moods and emotions which will set a right pattern, a constructive mood, for the rest of the day. Similarly, if someone else's conversation is full of negatives or anger or wrong attitudes, we can refuse to play that person's particular game and turn the conversation onto something that is wholesome, noble or constructive. We each have this ability to control what we take in and attend to. So we can teach the young the constructive powers of building their beliefs for themselves, and not to accept them second-hand from someone else.

Fifth, teach about visualisation, the awesome power of the pictures which we are carrying around daily in our heads. What can we do about them? When we want to lose weight, or improve our blood pressure, or develop our fitness, we simply go on a diet. We choose to eat certain things and to forgo others. The same principle holds with thoughts. We can make conscious choices to go without the things, the thoughts, the ideas which disturb and distract us. We can choose what we are going to give our attention to. Negative or poisonous thinking can be avoided in favour of embracing all the positive and wholesome things that come to our attention. We can erase negative and destructive talk from conversations, and introduce strongly positive and constructive topics to our thinking and speaking. We can re-track our thinking onto what is wholesome and balanced.

Success depends very strongly, we now realise, on language, especially upon picture-language, upon imagery. Our real intentions are implicit in the firmly held picture planted in our imagination. It is therefore worth considering the advice of that brilliantly insightful contemplative monk Carlo Carretto (1975; 170) who, following Kant, wrote:

> I have a secret I would like to share with you. . . . I have put it to the test time and time again. It goes like this: 'act as if'. . . . Are you in trouble and yet have the feeling that you do not have sufficient faith to cope with it? All right then, 'act as if' you did have faith, organise the details of your life as if you lived by faith. You will find that everything will work out in accordance with your desire for faith. . . . 'Act as if' you possessed. . . unbounded hope and endless charity, and cast yourself into the fray. . . . 'Act as if' . . . .

Sixth, give particular attention to visions of the future. How they conceive of the future is of fundamental importance to young people especially. So we have to ask what pictures of the future do we carry around in our heads? We should be careful, because they are about the future we will help to bring into existence. We all have expectations about our own immediate future (we sometimes call it ambition, or a career plan) and they tend to regulate our behaviours and choices. In most respects, then, we make up our minds what we want our world to be, and then select and reject opportunities according to that interior plan.

Seventh, distinguish between faith and hope. To say, 'I hope that so-and-so will happen' is a longing that has not yet quite become an expectation. But to say, 'So-and-so will happen' is an affirmation, a statement of confidence and conviction. Because, from all the evidence available, we can be convinced about it, we know that the creative powers of the universe, seen and unseen, will work together in harmony to convert that conviction into reality.

Eighth, tell stories, apocryphal stories. Stories are probably the most powerful teaching medium humankind has ever invented. Because we all take part in thousands if not millions of incidents throughout our lives, when we retell adventures, or relay an anecdote, we have invariably made a selection from a vast library of stories we could have told. If we listen to old people recalling their past, we find that they do not tell thousands of newly minted stories, but they tend to go back again and again to the same stories, the same incidents. Why? It is because they have made an implicit judgement about significance. These particular stories are to them in some way important, memorable, the conveyor of some significant message or messages. Recurrent stories are enormously important because they reveal the patterned way – indeed the pattern of the way – in which people conceive of their lives.

We ought to be attentive to what stories are told by a person, or by a group which shares an ideology, or within an organisation, or an ethnic group, particularly stories about the past and the future. What are being revealed in those tellings? In fact, are there common features, consistent underlying values, and recurrent imagery being used? All great religions abound in stories. They would never have survived unless they had discovered a means of conveying effectively the intangible, intellectually demanding value-frameworks to millions of relatively simple, uneducated adherents. Those shared belief systems become embodied in stories, often about the heroes, heroines and saints who have gone before them, and especially about the founder or founders. Sometimes, of course, we deliberately invent apocryphal stories, or fictions, or symbolical incidents to embody these meanings that 'lie too deep for tears'.

What stories, then, are we telling about our futures? There are many, in fact – from science fiction writers, from movies, from TV series. We do not often think of these as image-makers and the conveyors of values, but they are. They are the more important because they are shared; they give more than a private vision, but cultivate in a vast audience a 'way of seeing', so that millions of viewers are willing to suspend their disbelief for a period and to allow the persuasive coherence of this fabricated set of incidents to be entertained in every sense as a set of possibilities. Unfortunately, the dominant images of the future in our time are of disaster, decay and the progressive incorporation of human life into machine systems. So we need to pay attention to the often

hidden subtexts of stories and to ask if they are appropriate.
Stories can convey negative messages or they can help us to conceive of options worth striving for. So let us tell stories, positive
stories, about futures.

Ninth, teach and learn how to celebrate! In 1987 Harvard
University was 350 years old, and its alumni were invited to contribute to a celebratory fund. Alumni hardly needed to be told why
they should contribute; they only had to recall all the famous
people, ideas, books, discoveries and events which that great institution had contributed to the world. But alongside those shared
memories were a myriad other personal ones, of the incidents
(intellectual, social and spiritual), the friendships and contacts,
and the life-chances which any one of its graduates acquired there.
That 350th anniversary was worth celebrating, for the Latin
celebrare means to frequent, to visit often and to savour. Persons
who know how to celebrate are those who are capable of seeing
significance in what others might term ordinary.

Tenth, carefully select from, and use, the available tools. If there
is a single key to successful teaching about futures it is this. Tools
are basically enabling devices. They permit us to extend our
capacities and to create new things, new opportunities. The tools
of teaching and learning in a forward-looking manner are not new,
and they have been used in very many different contexts for more
than twenty years. We do need to be aware that appropriate
teaching methodologies are available, and several of them are
discussed below.

Every good teacher, every good school, every wise parent uses all
the devices suggested in these ten propositions. It does not surprise us, then, that at this particular point in our history, parents
are so insistent upon being given the right to choose their child's
school. Sometimes they are unclear why they want one school
rather than the next, but it has to do with sensing the balance,
wholeness, and health within it. They know there is a pervading
spirit to a school; they can smell, as it were, the milieu, the learning
environment, the way the students are valued, the value-set embedded in the syllabuses. Their intuition leads them to what is
'colligative' about the curriculum and the school that sponsors it.
An orientation about future possibilities pervades the warp and
woof of a good school's daily life.

SIX STRATEGIES FOR TEACHING ABOUT FUTURES

It is not possible to give a definitive list of teaching strategies which a teacher or parent may call upon, but we can illustrate several of the most promising. Six are given below as examples. Many others are accessible through works mentioned in the References at the back of this book.

Negotiating change by means of a cycle of transformation

It is regrettable that pundits, commentators, children's books and most media productions involving futures tend to focus on how technology will reconstruct external, tangible things in 'the future'. For underlying the surface of technical and economic change there are important human processes at work which have to do with transformations of meaning. To be aware of them is to open up new areas of enquiry and action and to create a new set of manifestations or externals.

Teachers are more aware than many that uncertainty, depression, frustration and fear often appear to be the dominant emotions of our times. A large number of the values and beliefs which have sustained the social landscape and gave it coherence have fallen, or are falling, apart. Work, leisure, defence, gender, progress, health and so on have lost much of their earlier significance and meanings. We are, in other words, living through a breakdown of inherited meanings. This is the first stage of a 'transformative cycle', or T-cycle for short (Figure 7.1).

The point is this: whereas unreflective immersion in the social dysfunctions of unemployment, stress, racism, crime, poverty and meaninglessness is certainly a cause for depression and anger, it is worth noting that aspects of the breakdown may be structural, resulting from forces in society rather than within individuals. While in fact the issues mentioned here raise the difficult question of personal versus individual responsibility, few would now see such concerns as merely the result of individual failure or bad luck. First, then, the T-cycle leads us to recognise a society-wide process which affects everyone and for which everyone is responsible. Second, we can begin to confront the depression or sense of guilt which results because, having brought the breakdown to full consciousness, we are now open to new choices and possibilities.

The recognition of the breakdown is a kind of ground-clearing

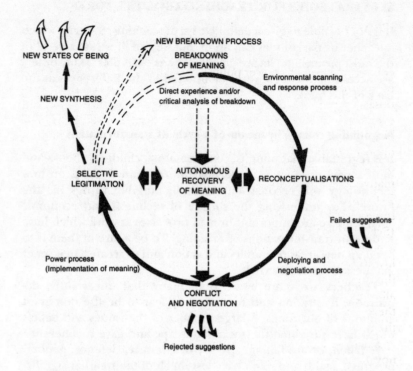

Figure 7.1 The transformation cycle

exercise, though in fact it is also continuous and parallels the other stages. It alerts us to search the cultural environment for anything which might be helpful in resolving the problem. Here we reach a second stage, in which we are engaged in evolving proposals, suggestions, or practices which explicitly address the breakdown.

Many people who put forward these reconceptualisations, or new proposals, would perhaps not think of themselves as involved in futures. Yet that is just what they are involved in, for in elaborating possible solutions they are setting up possibilities which invite individual and social responses. This process occurs in almost every conceivable area. Solution-oriented work never attracts much public attention, and some of it can lead to relatively trivial ends or to reality-avoidance. Many proposals simply fall by the wayside and are lost, and others fail because they are inappropriate or impractical. In any event, proposal-formation takes us on to the third stage.

Since far more proposals are fielded than can ever be taken up, some kind of winnowing process is needed. The sifting can of course be skewed by power politics, by lack of knowledge or by lack of appropriate forums in which they can be dicussed. New proposals often reach the stage of negotiations and conflicts without ever having had the benefit of wide public discussion. For example, when you think of the sheer effort and cost of mounting opposition to the siting of nuclear power stations, cruise missiles or a strategic military facility, it becomes immediately obvious why many social innovations seem to disappear without trace.

Conflicts occur because 'the new' impacts upon 'the old' and someone always has interests bound up in the way things were (Schon, 1971). The crucial capacity here is to be able to move from a position of open conflict to one of negotiation, and that shift involves organisation, support, commitment, a suitable arena and the equalisation of power relations (if only for the purposes of allowing discussion to proceed). To the extent that this occurs there is a chance for innovations to be taken up and legitimated, the final stage of the cycle.

Selective legitimation in Figure 7.1 refers to the way some innovations and proposals are accepted and incorporated in a new pattern. Examples are the emancipation of women, preventative health measures, smoke-free restaurants and nuclear-free zones. However, we cannot assume that the solutions which are accepted under present conditions are the right ones or the best available. Often they are not. Nevertheless this outline of the T-cycle does place in a sequence many of the activities which hitherto may have been considered in isolation. As a workshop method, teaching tool and research approach, the T-cycle has a variety of uses.

An assumption built into the T-cycle is that meanings, values, commitments and understandings have become less certain, more fluid and dynamic than perhaps they once were. Changes which once may have spanned centuries are now taking place in a few years. Since few schools were established with the express purpose of mediating change, it is not surprising that they find it hard to cope. Nor is it surprising that people exhibit symptoms of uncertainty, stress and fear as they regress to the 'minimal present'. However, longer-term views are attainable provided that the interpretive capacities involved are encouraged and developed. From within an 'extended present', the processes of continuity and change look less threatening. The key point is that those people who know that they stand at the centre of their own history as agents rather than as spectators are well placed to conceive of and imagine futures worth living in.

It is obviously unwise to skate over important questions about language, meaning, power and fundamentally conflicting interests. A more probing and critical approach provides access to meanings, commitments and understandings which tend to remain hidden precisely because they frame our world. It is often the taken-for-granted framework which is the problem, and thus the implicit content of official discourse may be more interesting than the explicit content. It is becoming increasingly clear that pictures about a future worth inhabiting are less likely to emerge from think-tanks and convocations of professional futurists than they will from the vision and determination of those who have learned to resist the hard sell and bland reassurances of experts.

Systematically dealing with fears

The Western world is caught within a profound dilemma. It has built a way of life which breaks with the past and yet it sustains few compelling visions of liveable futures. Deprived of roots and of direction, Western cultures exhibit a frantic presentness, a withdrawal to the 'here and now' in which the pain and conflict of mental/egoic life is partially assuaged by the marketing and consumption of substitute satisfactions, by avoidance. Far from embodying some higher vision of human life and purpose, contemporary culture exhibits many symptoms of a profound malaise: dissociation, regression, psychosis, paranoia. The most extreme of these symptoms is to be found in the existence, elaboration and deployment of nuclear weapons.

Nuclear weapons are the embodiment of technocratic barbarism. they are not simply an accidental side-effect or minor aberration: rather, they may be regarded as a consequence of an alienating mode of consciousness which has become split off from its human, environmental and spiritual sources through a long historical process. The fact that human life now appears to be framed within such cramped and indeed subhuman dimensions encourages a sense of importance and short-sightedness which particularly affects the young. As one researcher wrote:

a serious disillusionment is taking place – some children are reluctant to trust adults who are passing on to them such a dangerous and conflict-ridden world, whilst at the same time expecting children to behave peacefully. There is little incentive to grow up and every reason to dwell in the here-and-now, preferring whatever immediate and short-term pleasures and excitements are available.

(Davies, 1983)

Caught between an unrecognisable past and an unthinkable future, the present all too readily splinters into incoherent fragments: a mosaic of images, impressions, slogans and entertainments. Fears of nuclear devastation are reinforced by wider uncertainties about the development and control of other sophisticated technologies. In fact the latter have come to apppear so powerful, so determining of their social contexts, that many images of futures are largely images of possible future states of *things*, that is, of giant (or miniaturised) machines, cityscapes, arcologies, rocket ships, space stations, L-5 colonies and the like. This context presents the young with unprecedented challenges and dangers (Slaughter, 1991b). So dealing with fears becomes a priority. The following exercises are designed to begin that process. The first considers optimism and pessimism. The second uses a simple matrix to explore a range of responses to fears.

Optimism and pessimism

It has been suggested that optimists look forward to the future while pessimists cringe from it. It is possible to classify views of futures in such terms, but it gives rise to unnecessary polarities, to accounts of marvellous possibilities and terrifying disasters. The terms Utopia and Dystopia reflect these extremes. In the post-war period more images of future disasters have been produced than the opposite.

But this division between optimism and pessimism is not quite as simple as it seems. It is true that pessimism may lead to despair, but it may also stimulate a person to search for effective solutions. On the other hand, optimism can leave an individual's energy free for constructive projects or it may encourage bland, unhelpful, business-as-usual attitudes. In both cases the human response is crucial. Optimism and pessimism can both inhibit or encourage effective responses. The crucial factor, then, is not the object of attention but the quality of understanding, the quality of response, brought to bear upon it.

Here then is an exercise which represents one way of dealing constructively with a person's fears about futures. Students can consider the following questions and begin to explore their own feelings and responses. A simple lead-in, appropriate for younger students, is to build familiarity with 'plus or minus' words, 'positive and negative' words and finally, responses which 'encourage' or 'hold back' (see Figure 7.2). Here are some possible questions for students to use.

1 What makes you feel optimistic about the future and why? What effect does this have upon you?
2 What makes you feel pessimistic about the future and why? Outline the effect this has upon you.
3 Using your answers to 1 and 2, fill in the matrix. What can you conclude about your responses from the completed matrix?
4 What strategies could you adopt which would alter your responses or change the existing balance between enabling and inhibiting outcomes?

Events or possibilities	Optimistic response		Pessimistic response	
	Holds back	Encourages	Holds back	Encourages
e.g. School exams	Over-confidence	Works even harder to get distinction	Resignation to the inevitable	Makes up lost ground

Figure 7.2 Optimism and pessimism

Dealing with negative images of futures

This exercise was developed to help teachers and secondary students explore their responses to feared futures. Its purpose is two-fold – first to place negative images and fears in a wider context; second, to draw attention to high quality responses. It is usually best to precede the exercise with a careful consideration of what students fear. They can then be taken through the process and encouraged to invent some 'high quality' responses in relation to the focus they have chosen.

Students begin by focusing upon something which directly concerns them. They are asked to hold the images, feelings, associations and so on out before them in a relaxed and non-judgmental way. They can then begin to explore possible responses as suggested by the matrix (see Figure 7.3). There are four categories which they can use, each corresponding to a cell in the matrix: acceptance and low quality responses; acceptance and high quality responses; rejection and low quality responses; rejection and high quality responses.

1 There should now be up to four sets of strategies for dealing with the issue. Can they be placed in order of priority?
2 Is there a clear 'best' solution? (There may be valuable elements in one or more of the strategies which could be combined in a number of ways.)

	Low quality responses	High quality responses
Acceptance of negative images		
Rejection of negative images		

Figure 7.3 A matrix for responding to fears

3 What resources, changes, commitments and support are needed to put the preferred strategy into practice?

The characteristics of high-quality responses can be brought to students' attention, and there is an enormous range to choose from. It can be pointed out that most fears are overstated or illusory. Images of the future are *provisional* and *negotiable*. They represent opportunities for engagement, choice, action. Images of the future are just that – images, potentials, possibilities. They arise from and depend upon human vision and perception. The locus of power therefore resides in people and not in the image. A high quality response is an imaginative response. It has the capacity to go beyond the given. It is creative.

Imaging futures

Images of futures are much more important than is commonly realised. They powerfully affect what people believe and do in the present, and they are continuously being negotiated at all levels of society. Large and powerful organisations have long realised the force of images and have assimilated aspects of planning and forecasting into their public relations activities. Thus some forms of futures research have become associated with the interests of such groups with the result that partial, or biased, views of futures are sometimes presented as if they are natural and inevitable extensions of the present.

Teachers and parents in particular will find it useful to bear in mind that whenever images of futures are presented as non-negotiable or finished, they are likely to conceal an attempt to persuade by stealth and to secure one set of interests at the expense of others. This process of mystification becomes visible in some educational debates when a preferred form of society is accorded uncritical prominence. Such strategies implicitly cast individuals in the role of helpless bystanders: observers of, rather than participants in, the historical process. But teachers do not need to accept a passive role for themselves or their pupils. They can begin to explore and analyse images of futures, identify the interests they represent, develop their own vision and explore commonalities with others. In these and other ways they may promote active, responsible notions of citizenship which encourage people to participate in creating the future they want rather than the ones which flow from remote and impersonal forces. Here is one way of introducing the theme of imaging futures.

An imaging workshop on inventing liveable futures

Most images of futures, paradoxically, are products of the past. In this exercise the aim is to let go of the past and to make a leap toward a future state which is a product of one's own will and design. Any focus can be selected so long as it is one which inspires the participants. The images we invent are acts of discovery and purpose. Properly used they can open out new possibilities for action and change. The images may be purely personal or shared with others – for example, envisioning a world without weapons (see Boulding, 1988). It is worth taking time to explore this process properly; in fact, it is enhanced by devoting to it at least a whole morning or afternoon. The environment should be quiet and supportive. Art materials should be at hand and sensitive facilitation is essential. While an in-depth workshop may extend over a couple of days, a shorter version for use in classrooms can be derived from the following steps.

1 Decide on the focus and the purpose of the exercise.
2 Situate it in a specific future time – say 20 to 40 years ahead.
3 Help students to relax and be there in that future. Allow them to *remember* their preferred image(s) of that future world.
4 Next, allow the image(s) to become specific and concrete.
5 The images are then outlined as clearly as possible. They can take the form of a written description, a drawing, a design or simply a mind image.
6 The image is described to a partner who listens passively. The partner helps to nurture the image by asking questions which allow students to be clearer, more concrete and specific. Criticism plays no part in this process.
7 Participants begin to explore the meaning of the preferred future together. They tease out central themes and compelling images.
8 If there is time, the consequences of different futures are examined via a futures wheel – the title of a future is placed at the centre of a large, blank piece of paper, and some of the likely spin-offs and their consequences are then traced out like spokes radiating from that centre.

9 Students now think about this future. How did it happen? Discourage use of the future tense; it *has* happened, so the idea is to look back and 'remember' how.

10 Once the main features of this process have been noted they can be translated back into the real present. Some of the short-term objectives which lead in the direction of a scenario can be worked out.

11 Finally, there is a search for points of leverage, action settings key people and resources which could help to bring that pre-ferred future into being.

12 Steps 5 to 11 can be repeated with a partner. The result should be a number of well worked-out views of futures which have been consciously chosen, elaborated and linked with the present.

Various criticisms of this workshop process can be made. For example, if it has been poorly done it can lead to naive castles in the air, or simple wish fulfilment. The links back to the present may not be carefully delineated, leaving the vision dangling and disconnected. The nurturing and supporting of images may not be enough to render them sufficiently real. However, the workshop approach is useful for helping us to look beyond the limitations of present structures and present paradigms of enquiry. It allows individuals to consider possibilities which may never before have been brought to mind and considered properly. It provides a way of escaping imaginatively from the temporary constraints of life now, and of conceptualising other, divergent options.

Explore the extended present

The English language separates past, present and future into three distinct tenses. Some of the meanings associated with the tenses are as follows:

Past   history, experience, memory, identity, upbringing, achievements.

Present   the here and now, the fleeting moment, the focus of attention.

Future   images, intentions, purposes, projects, plans, hopes, fears.

The point here is subtle but very important. The past, present and future have to be distinguishable one from the other, but they cannot be separated. The boundaries between them are fluid. Past events affect the present and future; present perceptions, choices and actions draw on past knowledge and flow forward to affect the future. The futures which become our present develop from both short-term and long-term processes. And we are all involved. Decisions to opt out are decisions nonetheless and they have consequences.

The human body is obviously restricted to a fairly narrow present, but the mind, imagination and spirit can range out over immense areas of space and time. The diagram in Figure 7.4 takes up this idea and suggests that the present cannot be understood simply as a fixed period of time. The question 'How long is the present?' can be answered in the following way: 'It may be short or long depending upon how it is understood, and by whom'.

As we noted in the previous chapter, if the mental present has no firm boundaries, it follows that in each situation we can exercise a choice about the time-frame we adopt. For example, to drive a car requires a very narrow, close-up time-frame, which is adequate for making split-second judgments. On the other hand, at the level of cultural and ecological processes we are clearly making decisions which can impact over many thousands of years. This flexible time-frame, open to our choice, creates something of a dilemma: given the unknown dimensions of the future, how can we determine an appropriate time-frame for education?

Boulding's notion of a 200-year present puts us in touch with our recent origins and also with the immediate consequences of our actions and decisions. It is literally our temporal context, one

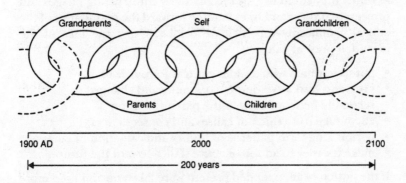

Figure 7.4 The extended present – a family chain

which requires us neither to dig into the remote past nor to peer into the distant future. We are connected to this span of time in many ways, but not least through the lives of our families (particularly of our grandparents and our grandchildren). The notion of reconnecting to a wider world of significance, or process, or interaction is perhaps one of the most fruitful and productive ways of moving beyond the world-view of the industrial era. This is a very simple idea. Yet the more people have worked with it, the more useful it has appeared.

If the notion of an extended present became more widely used, it would impact upon a variety of meanings and practices and permit a reframing of the temporal context for many human activities. Imagine the shifts which would occur in economics if future-discounting rates were substantially revised. Consider how our use of the environment might change. Or think of how the curricula in schools would change if they had to reflect *both* halves of this period. That all this emerges from just one concept demonstrates how productive the elaboration of futures concepts can be.

We can therefore conclude that futures concepts are as important as methodologies and they can be employed in many different subject areas. How can this one of the two-hundred-year present be put to use in schools? Figure 7.4 shows a chain of family relationships drawn from the viewpoint of our own time. The links in this chain are the people who have lived before us and those who will live after. Some of the people in our past can be consulted directly, through studying their possessions or by reading the histories of the experiences of their generation. The people of our future can also be considered by anticipating the future conditions in which they could live, by imaginatively constructing images and projects of futures and by extending forward the boundaries of the ethical community to which we belong. Using the idea of the extended present can

- put us in touch with a wider context for our lives;
- provide a bird's-eye view of continuity and change;
- relate the here-and-now to the past and future;
- encourage us to think of causes and consequences;
- permit long-term patterns of history and causation to emerge;
- make it easier to adopt an active stance toward the future.

If the notion of an extended present were taken up and used more widely, if it were adopted as a standard operating assumption or as a regular teaching method, it could affect the way people think about the world and the way they make decisions. For example, many long-term problems arise simply because people discount the future. Short-term thinking considers only the immediate and close-up effects of actions and decisions. The longer-term implications are therefore minimised or ignored.

The use of a longer time-frame would have tangible results in areas like the following:

- the management of tropical forests and of other fragile habitats;
- the conceptualisation and management of pollution; and of petroleum and fossil-fuel reserves;
- the nature of the built environment;
- mining and manufacturing;
- wildlife conservation and the uses of the environment.

To summarise; 'the present' can mean many things depending upon the activities, purposes and perceptions with which we are involved at the time. The 'extended present' is a very powerful notion. If we choose to acknowledge our debt to the past and our responsibilities toward the future, such a notion could restore some of the important connections which exist between them. It follows that this wider notion of the present is likely to become part of any sustainable world view.

Students can explore different notions of the present by considering questions such as those which follow.

1 Try to answer the following questions: How old is language? How far into the future do present decisions extend? How long is the present for (a) a racing driver, (b) an artist, (c) an architect and (d) a mystic?
2 The 200-year present stretches some hundred years in each direction. What are the possible benefits and drawbacks of this idea?
3 Interview some elderly people and fill in the first half of the 200-year present as fully as possible. What does this suggest about the second half of 'the present'?
4 Explore the notion of a self-fulfilling prophecy – how we create things the way we expect them to be. How does it work? Are there any major costs involved?
5 The idea of a bounded present has a number of important drawbacks. What are some of them?

6 Outline an argument for inventing new words to describe the links between past, present and future. Coin some terms which you consider to be suitable for wider use. Explain your choices.

Looking for solutions in the right places

One of the notable things about many futures-related issues and problems is that solutions are seldom available on the level at which they are first experienced or understood. Consider two examples. The first involves a child's response to some gross act of pollution. Commonly children react with concern, anger or outrage. Yet what can they actually do? At best their responses may contribute to some local action which may possibly deal with local sources of pollution. But they feel, and are, helpless to change the way that Western cultures have abused the environment. A second example is that of the householder who finds that a replacement part for a kitchen appliance is unavailable. What to do? Unless one is fortunate enough to know a mechanic with access to outdated spares, one usually has to junk the item and buy a new one. Many adults resent 'planned obsolescence' and the forced expenditures it imposes. They feel manipulated by something beyond their control. And they are!

In these cases (and in countless others) individuals confront the outward manifestations of an embedded culture and world-view which are not susceptible to direct pragmatic action. This is made clearer by reference to Figure 7.5. Here three levels of analysis are outlined: the litany (problems as experienced directly); social practice (the structures, interactions and practices of social life); and world-view (the underlying constitutive modes of understanding). At level One it is hard to see how any real changes can be conceived of or implemented since one is basically locked

The litany: population, resources, environment (pop futurism, problem-focused futures work)

Social practice: laws, rules, regulations, structures, procedures, forecasting, planning (futures within the status quo)

World-view: constitutive understandings, norms, presuppositions, cultural 'givens' (critical and epistemological futures study)

Figure 7.5 Levels of analysis

in to a dominant status quo. Level Two gives access to more useful options: the framing of new laws, the imposition of new rules, the implementation of new planning procedures. Yet work here may be subverted if it stands in opposition to the underlying structures of meaning at level Three. It is here that the most powerful options for change arise because it is here that our understandings of the world take shape.

For example, conservationists operating at level One have fought a long series of largely unsuccessful rearguard actions against economic and population growth. Social activists have acted more effectively at level Two to ban, for example, the use of certain pesticides, the hunting of whales, or drift-net fishing. But it is the thorough-going cultural critique of 'progress', 'growth', the definition of nature as 'resources', for example, that lead on to the possibility of adaptive cultural innovation. Hence, it is not so much in protests at level One, or activism at level Two that the real hope of the future lies. Critical analysis of the hidden commitments of the industrial world-view expose the partiality of that world-view and the real alternatives to it.

As noted above, Ruth Benedict suggested that 'no man ever sees the world through pristine eyes. He sees it edited by a definite set of customs and institutions and ways of thinking' (Benedict, 1935; 1961: 2). This analysis therefore leads toward some powerful strategies for responding to a world in transition: cultural editing, the framing of alternatives and social innovations.

Cultural editing refers to the ways a particular tradition encourages favoured ways of seeing and knowing. This book has explored some of the drawbacks of that process in industrialised contexts. Teachers who wish to consider these processes with their students may take some of the themes we have mentioned, like growth, the loss of a sense of limits, nature as a thing or a resource, the authority of the past, and loss of the numinous (or inner quality of things). Each of these may be traced from their hidden sources in the world-view to the social practices which they permit and the problems which have resulted.

A next step is to consider the framing of cultural alternatives based on different assumptions and meanings, a step which leads to a series of very interesting questions. What would a culture based on a different model of rationality look like? How would we relate to nature (and each other) if we felt deeply interconnected with it? How would we act if we believed in safeguarding the rights of future generations? What innovations would foresight cultures implement? How would economics change if intrinsic value (rather than use, or exchange value) were a basic operating assumption? Such questions are more than simple mind games. They tap the most powerful options for change available to us. As such they can be placed firmly on the educational agenda.

Clearly, social innovations of many kinds can spring from this kind of approach, but not all such innovations need to be so profound. The Institute for Social Inventions exists to encourage ordinary people to be creative in everyday contexts. It has published a catalogue of new ideas, both theoretical and applied, which show the range of possibilities (Albery and Yule, 1989). Such sources provide a good starting point for answering the often-asked question, 'What can I do?'

Answering the 'What can I do?' question

For reasons given above, many young people feel disempowered in the face of nuclear weapons, unemployment, environmental decline and other grave threats. But we have shown that there are many answers to this question. They include:

- understanding change;
- developing quality responses to fears and concerns;
- using workshop methods to develop images of futures; and
- considering solutions at various levels.

We can now reintegrate some of this material in a slightly different way and, in so doing, provide a general strategy for dealing with change, for empowering students and for providing quality answers to their questions. The summary statement for this approach is to say that 'the answer is a journey'. What does this mean?

The journey we are referring to is simultaneously one of self-discovery and one of external exploration. The self-discovery part is about finding out who one really is. Another term is 'vocation' (literally, a calling) and this is a world away from a narrow, imposed vocationalism. It has to do with the skills and disciplines of quiet listening and reflection. The important thing is to look and listen in the right ways, and to learn this craft one should ideally ask those who are already good at it; there are many capable people who can help others find their vocation.

The external exploration is a search for materials, resources, concepts and understandings through which to make sense of the world. Most of the knowledge will already exist, and those who persist in looking tend to find what they need. Hence a slightly expanded answer to the question 'What can I do?' could be something like this: 'You could embark on a journey of inner and outer discovery. As you do so you will find everything you need, including the nature of the projects you could undertake and any associates you may need to help you'. In our view this is a reasonable answer. It is helpful, but non-directive. We can now summarise this process in a number of distinct stages or steps:

• Focus on a particular issue, problem, or concern.
• Research the problem. Can it be redefined? What foundation is it resting upon? Who else has worked, or is working, in the area? At what levels can the problem be addressed and understood?
• Consider a range of solutions. Does any particular avenue of enquiry or action stand out? If so, why? Has it been tried before? Do any proposed solutions deal with the problem in depth?
• Note that the act of focusing on solutions is important in its own right, because whatever we focus upon grows. This is a very powerful process and many creative people use it: first a sketch or an outline idea is produced; next, a provisional structure is created; the structure is then tested, refined and completed.
• Finally, it is helpful to realise that this problem-solving process always takes place in a social context. The T-cycle sketched in some aspects of that context. However, it is important to note that when people ask 'What can I do?' questions, they are not standing alone, but that they are surrounded by helpful resources. This is particularly true of the symbolic and methodological resources found in the futures field, as is shown in Figure 7.6.

APPLYING THE BRIDGING STRATEGIES

There are many points in schools and schooling where these kinds of strategies can be applied in order to bridge the divide between an obsolescent world-view and an emerging one; and teachers will easily find opportunities to embed these approaches in their work. To demonstrate how to apply the bridging strategies, let us consider three loci in educational systems: the system level; the school or institution level; and the level of the individual learner or

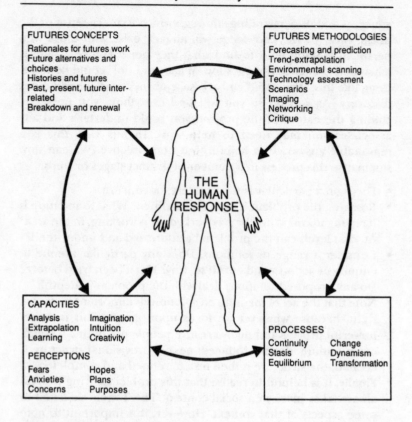

FUTURES CONCEPTS
Rationales for futures work
Future alternatives and
choices
Histories and futures
Past, present, future inter-
related
Breakdown and renewal

FUTURES METHODOLOGIES
Forecasting and prediction
Trend-extrapolation
Environmental scanning
Technology assessment
Scenarios
Imaging
Networking
Critique

THE
HUMAN
RESPONSE

CAPACITIES
Analysis   Imagination
Extrapolation   Intuition
Learning   Creativity

PERCEPTIONS
Fears   Hopes
Anxieties Plans
Concerns   Purposes

PROCESSES
Continuity   Change
Stasis   Dynamism
Equilibrium   Transformation

Figure 7.6 What can I do?

teacher. A brief review of some of the options at each level will
serve to summarise the views outlined in this chapter.

The system level

The key question to ask here is whether there is a strategic planning
process in place. It must be a process which is proactive, set up, that
is, to read the signals of change, to explore alternatives and to develop
strategic options. The QUEST (Quick Environmental Scanning
Technique) approach can be successfully applied in educational
organisations at this, and at the institutional, level. It requires that the
most senior decision-makers meet for two intensive workshops during
which their expert knowledge is tapped, systematically evaluated,

and then built up into a composite picture of what the organisation looks like in its environment. Scenarios are developed and strategic options suitable for each are developed. This avoids the need to forecast or predict which future will actually happen. Options are then sought which seem to apply across the range of scenarios. In this way a forward-looking decision context is developed which provides a basis for strategic decision-making (Slaughter, 1990a).

Another important initiative at the system level is to ensure that there is institutional support for forward-looking innovation. Suitable curriculum materials, opportunities for professional development, consultant advice, and access to specialist expertise are needed here, although these services do not have to be provided from within the system itself; but the means must exist to access them. Education systems have been relatively slow to pick up and use the available tools, whereas government, business and industry have used some of them for many decades. Perhaps such tardiness is evidence of how deeply education systems have been immersed in the past and the short-term present.

The school or institution

At this level, all the staff should be thinking about how to introduce futures-related content and methodology into every aspect of the life of the school, and especially into classrooms. The task is one which usually would fall to the Principal, curriculum co-ordinators and faculty heads, although, in the light of the discussion in chapter 5 about post-bureaucratic organisations, we should wonder whether a school which is hierarchically ordered like this is adequately structured for the new approach and whether its very shape tends to contradict what it is attempting to do. In the same way, futures ought not to be considered a new subject, though it can be treated as such. It is better seen as a cross-curricular dimension, a kind of pervasive style which penetrates all curriculum offerings.

Most schools have the opportunity to include a variety of futures-related perspectives in their special projects. Indeed, celebrations like a Whole Earth Day, and information evenings where parents can be introduced to the new frameworks and methods are worthy of consideration. McDonagh's *To Care for the Earth* gives some examples of how he attempted within his church to develop ceremonies compatible with the new world-view. In the same way, schools need to ask themselves what priorities are being evoked in ceremonies like assemblies which are regularly held in the school.

The individual teacher

Since education is by its very nature a forward-looking enterprise with interests in the development of individual people, in their employment, in their personal well-being and in the future development of society, every teacher needs to understand how to deal with the futures-related aspects of his or her work. While it may not be necessary for all teachers to be specialists in futures or to be skilled with the kinds of tools and strategies which have been discussed above, it is of fundamental importance that every teacher is aware how, in the daily fabric of the classroom and in the routine functions of the school, a world-view is given a habitation and a name. There is already a world-view underlying everything the school attempts to do. Is it good enough? Is it obsolescent? How can it be refined or changed?

It is likely that the great majority of teachers are unfamiliar with the substantial literature dealing with futures. There is a core of perhaps two hundred quality works which ought to form the heart of preservice preparation for teachers. The material presented in this book shows the urgency of having every teacher prepared to operate in a paradigm which supersedes industrialism, disconnectedness and mere positivism. Nothing less than the survival of life on earth depends on it. Although teachers may feel that they are non-specialists in this area, they ought to be at least acquainted with the new paradigm's perspectives and overviews; its concepts, metaphors and methodologies; with how to cope with futures issues and concerns; with how images about futures and school practices interact; with the ideas being produced by writers like Drexler (on nanotechnology), Reanney (on the 'death of forever'), Berry (on 'bioregional stories'), and Bohm (on the 'implicate order'). Every teacher should know about this literature, even if he or she reads only a small part of it.

Beyond the literature there are networks, organisations and professional associations which are active on a global scale. The resources available in the futures field are more than ample to support the work of teachers, and those who are responsible for an education which can invest the new century with promise rather than foreboding. Confronted by the urgency of making education responsive to futures considerations, we now attempt to answer some of the questions most commonly asked by teachers and parents about schools and futures.

SOME QUESTIONS ABOUT SCHOOLS AND FUTURES

How does one get hold of the concept of futures when the concept itself seems elusive?

It may seem elusive at first because futures perspectives have not been highlighted in our training or culture. It is at base a question of familiarity. As one reads into, and reflects upon, substantive futures work the picture becomes much clearer. The field has a functional and a conceptual structure which can be explored and applied via specific concepts, theories, approaches, and methodologies. The usual pattern is for people to experience some initial puzzlement. But this soon passes as the material becomes more familiar. Before long, a number of welcome consequences emerge. They include: a renewal of qualified optimism, a newly created perspective and access to new personal and professional options. Above all, start to read, and be aware that your own worldview may be in need of some radical revisions.

It is difficult to plan for the future if you cannot predict what the future will bring. To what extent does avoiding prediction present a conceptual difficulty?

It is not possible to avoid prediction entirely. Many 'weak' predictions must be made in the conduct of everyday life as well as in all the assumptions which must be made when planning or otherwise looking ahead. But these informal acts should not be confused with the 'strong' or 'hard' predictions which apply to systems which can be fully measured and quantified. Hence it is possible to predict birthdays, eclipses and the general performance of technical systems; but human actions and social futures are inherently uncertain and therefore less predictable. Since futures cannot be predicted in any absolute sense, planning has shifted toward understanding and responding to change. The emphasis has moved away from forecasting with accuracy and towards modes of responding to constant change.

If futures are not predictable, how do you respond to trends?

It depends upon what the trends are. If they are welcome, one may elect to support them. If they are unwelcome one can choose to work against them. Trends are always provisional; there is an aphorism which goes, 'A trend is not destiny'. We therefore ought to be suitably questioning about 'megatrends', which run the risk of being an over-simplification and of producing reified view of the future. Since the study of anything is never 'value-free', one should always remain properly skeptical of the basis from which trends are derived. As with forecasts, one should consider carefully the underlying assumptions and data-base before giving credence to any trend.

What can you 'know' about futures without predicting?

You can build up knowledge of contexts, changes, processes and alternatives from which the future will emerge. A lot of futures work is about the elaboration of particular scenarios. When a number of these projected events are compared, they reveal alternatives which invite choices in the present. In other words, futures work sets up a decision context which is continually supplemented and revised by new events and new information. Hence, knowledge about 'the future' is always provisional, always in the process of development. Indeed, our plans, purposes, goals, intentions, images and the like are 'read upon' the future and affect both it and the moving present. There are no future facts *per se*. But the careful elaboration of futures potentials gives us a range of high-quality material to work with. Thus, far from being 'an empty space' the future is more like an imaginative and intellectual realm which is anything but empty.

To what extent is the futures agenda being set by big business?

To a considerable extent. It is being set by the direct and continuous impact of advertising and commercial values, by the close connections between governments and corporations and also by the fact that large businesses are the major employers of futures people. Much high-quality work is carried out by futures researchers for large corporations, but this work is seldom made available to, say, the public or to educational systems. In part this is because they have not demanded it! On the other hand, some firms are secretive and use this work to advance their own, limited interests (for example, in marketing). Hence there is a constant need (*a*) to provide critiques of corporate assumptions, values and work; and (*b*) to pursue non-commercial approaches in the broader public interest. But it is important to keep reminding yourself that everything written about the future and about the present is predicated on a system of beliefs, a paradigm, a 'way of knowing' and we owe it to ourselves to critique those funda-mental assumptions. We do not have to accept someone else's agenda.

It does not seem possible to slow down the rate of change. How, then, can we heal the past when the processes which are causing damage are accelerating?

It is a mistake to see change processes as abstract imperatives which cannot be influenced by human actions. Most processes of change are the direct result of someone's action, though the latter may be hidden by such factors as time, distance or the mysti-fications of ideological discourse. 'Accelerating change' is a result of forces created by human effort in response to national competit-iveness, technical innovation, the profit motive, the imperatives of capitalist values and practices, and so on. The world has become steadily coopted into this compulsive and seemingly unstoppable process. However, when the destructive consequences of the process are understood and brought to full consciousness, such changes can be challenged, redirected or halted. It is therefore entirely possible to engage in healing the past while at the same time working to delegitimise destructive change.

If schools mirror social values, how can they change society in a way which will guarantee preferable futures?

By small changes in desired directions. While it is true that schools cannot move too far ahead of their social contexts, they constitute one of the main social institutions with a special responsibility to look ahead and to take a longer view. Education necessarily in-volves making assumptions about futures and it helps in funda-mental ways to create them. Hence teachers should be fully aware of how futures approaches contribute to the educational process.

They also need to explain this aspect of their work to parents and other constituencies. Schools can take on a leadership role when this role clearly involves acting responsibly and in the interests of present and future generations. Such leadership can tap legitimate but not clearly articulated community concerns, much as the environmental issue has. The key is to be very clear about underlying rationales, and to communicate them well.

Some media commentators present depressing scenarios. What positive support can one find for teaching futures, and how can one gain access to the right people?

Positive support can be found in the life and work of many active and committed people. Their examples can be studied and emulated. On a more practical level, schools can subscribe to the relevant publications and organisations in the futures area. For those who are teaching futures, the World Futures Studies Federation is a truly international network of practitioners, providing access to many key people in this field. Courses on futures and futures in education are taught at a number of universities around the world. There are also a number of local organisations and networks.

But one should not overlook one's closest colleagues. There already is a values framework at work in your school, and it affects all those cultural aspects of schooling which we alluded to in chapter 5. So critique your own school; where does it stand on the issues which formed the subject of chapters 2, 3 and 4?

There are social movements which lead toward a positive future. But what about other movements (such as the Islamic fundamentalists) who seem to move away from hope and lead us deeper into crisis?

They represent a very real challenge and perhaps danger. However, the fact that a danger is recognised is the first step towards dealing with it. For example, concerned Americans pursued a deliberate strategy of 'citizen diplomacy' with people in the Soviet Union and have arguably been a factor in ending the cold war. Given appropriate foresight and personal dedication, such work could be repeated elsewhere. However, there are no guarantees. Crises sometimes constitute extremely costly social learning experiences, the consequences of which are largely unpredictable.

Will our present lack of control over events and processes force change upon us, making it impossible to work toward a preferred future?

Change is forced upon us only when we have failed to read the warning signs and to act in time. This is already the case with the premature extinction of many species of wildlife, of clear-felled forests and other ruined ecosystems. However, the degree of control available always depends upon agendas, priorities and choices. Hence it is not true that we 'lack control'. By exercising foresight we can do more than merely avoid undesirable outcomes; we can activate choices and work toward preferred ends. But there is no guarantee that we will succeed in any particular case. Foresight greatly increases our ability to direct and decide, but it is not foolproof, nor is it universally applied. So, while our path into the future remains dangerous and uncertain, it is always possible (and necessary) to work toward preferred ends.

Does technology define our existence?

Many believe that it does, but the apparent supremecy of technology and its instrumental mode of rationality are not things to be passively accepted. There are powerful reasons for believing that technology can, and should, be given a less dominant place in a reconstructed worldview which re-establishes other, more important aspects of the human and social context.

Given the fact of social and value pluralism and the lack of a common philosophy, how can we find a common agenda or direction?

Pluralism need not be a problem if some underlying commonalities of interest can be defined and safeguarded. It is entirely possible that common interests in peace, a healthy environment, social justice will establish themselves as items on the human and cultural agenda for the twenty-first Century. Human variability can flourish and develop in many different ways which need not put at risk the agreed agenda.

How can one empower students and young people?

By allowing them to admit their fears and concerns, but then to focus in depth on exploring responses to them. Teachers can help students to work through their responses if they use methods like workshops, various approaches to creativity, writing autobiographies, teaching reflection and by studying the examples of people who used their lives to bring about important and progressive changes.

What role does the religious or spiritual dimension play?

The external (or exoteric) forms of religion are not particularly useful when they lack a strong spiritual component. When this condition is fulfilled, new principles and powers come into play which are permanently capable of transcending every problem and all catastrophes, real or imagined. This is so because, while technology creates new devices, new rules, spiritual development creates higher-order realities. In a properly differentiated universe, spiritual knowing occupies the highest ontological level and manifests emergent qualities which are quite literally unavailable on other levels. Spiritual growth and development therefore offer us the most powerful and creative human options. These in turn allow us to envision and to create futures which go a very long way beyond those imaginable from within an industrial, a technological or a materialist world-view.

Conclusion
The promise of the twenty-first century

During the present transition period, nightmare-like fantasies have become socialized and thereby sanctioned as acceptable parts of national and international life. Civilisations have been trying to hold the violent manifestations of these fantasies in their lairs, with moderate success. But modern technology, communication, and social advances themselves helped lift the lid off the inner turmoils of people, allowing the reptile mind to act out its desires.

J. T. Fraser, *Time the Familiar Stranger*, 1987

It is quite possible for a project of global restoration to emerge into the world culture before the end of the present century; possible for a message to go out through the mass media about the first human project, a common effort to repair the foundations of all our lives.

Walter Anderson, *To Govern Evolution*, 1987

The end of one millenium and the prospect of another to follow is not merely symbolic; it provides an opportunity to take stock and consider our position. Why are such turning points important? They reflect two powerful aspects of our reality. One is the capacity (or rather the need) of the human mind to move at will through time past, present and future. The other is the fact of our interconnectedness with all things past and future.

During the course of everyday life we become entrained in short-term, ego-bound thinking, in the limited demands of a present conceived minimally as 'the here and now.' But the transition into a new century reminds us, as few other events can, of the wider process which willy-nilly we participate in. Looking back over the last hundred years we contemplate our roots in the lives and cultures of our parents and their parents. Looking forward over the next hundred years we open with our children, and theirs, to the world which is growing organically, day by day, from this moment. This 200-year present is our space in time. And when we reach the changeover, as dictated by the calendar and our numbering system, for a brief moment we seem to stand on a pivot of history.

The perspective catches our imagination. It is, perhaps, the temporal equivalent of the view from a high mountain. The details which had absorbed us stand revealed in a breathtaking panorama. The daily routine, all routines and patterns, fit seamlessly into a vaster landscape. The micro blends into the macro and they into the cosmic. Scales merge into each other. Nothing is separate. Yet that is where the analogy ends. For we are keenly aware that the twentieth century has been harrowing for us, for the Earth and indeed for our children.

It is highly significant that at the end of the nineteenth century people looked ahead with optimism and hope. They believed that the rational application of scientific knowledge and technical skill would remake the world and usher in an era of peace and prosperity. Nowadays it takes a profound act of historical imagination to reconstruct that same sense of boundless possibility, for we carry with us the experience of the souring of the dream: of wars, catastrophes and the steady deterioration of our prospects and our images of the future. It is a heavy burden. One of the hidden resistances to studying futures is the repression of this knowledge, the avoidance both of mortality and of our responsibilities to future generations (Reanney, 1991; Busuttil, 1990).

But approaching the new millenium we know at a deep, incontrovertible level that everything is at stake. As Macy puts it:

> with isolated exceptions, every generation prior to ours has lived with the assumption that other generations would follow. . . . Now we have lost the certainty that we will have a future. I believe this loss, felt at some level of consciousness by everyone, regardless of political orientation, is the pivotal psychological reality of our time.
>
> (Macy, 1991: 5)

There is no transcendent principle which says that the experiment of life on planet Earth must succeed. Our very success as a species, coupled with the extraordinary assumptions and habits of the industrial era, have brought us to a real 'hinge in history', not an imaginary one, nor merely a calendar change. So it is not surprising that people have come to fear the future as though it were a disaster that has already happened. To the extent that substances such as plutonium will be around for up to 250,000 years, that the viability of forests and other ecosystems is threatened or that some powerful new technology may undermine everything, this could be true. However, we have explored the grounds of a different view.

We maintained above that the future cannot be predicted precisely because people are active agents in shaping and creating history. This very fact, which to the uninformed view seems to imperil the futures enterprise, actually conceals the very principle which shows the way beyond our dilemma. For it is possible that a keen awareness of both halves of this two-hundred year period may stimulate changes, shifts of perception, processes and actions which, taken together, could lead in an entirely different direction. The basic suggestion of this book is that the human response (in every sense of that term) is of primary significance. That is why we can be hopeful and guardedly optimistic while also feeling deeply the tragedy of the times in which we live.

There is, of course, a danger in wishful thinking, of finding good in everything, a silver lining in every cloud. But that is not what we are suggesting. We are indeed in very great peril. But, properly handled, that fact may jolt us into a new awareness of where we are, of who we are and what we need to do. Empowerment springs, in part, from a developing congruence of insight about such things. It is most emphatically not a case of thinking good thoughts and being good, positive people. There are times when we may need to get angry! We are not recommending quietism. The point is that we face a challenge of unprecedented proportions. It is a challenge which goes to the very heart of schooling and education, and we have known it for some time. But late industrial cultures have provided so many diversions and avoidance strategies that most of us are simply not paying attention. Therein lies the real tragedy.

The approach of a new century provides a genuine chance to take stock. We have looked back at the horrors of the time: at Auschwitz, Hiroshima, Bhopal and the rest. We have looked right into the abyss – and then beyond it to the processes of recovery and renewal which point in quite different directions. This is not an illusion. We have shown that there is plenty of evidence that *within the vast span of human cultures and responses there can be found all the resources necessary to reconceptualise our predicament and steer in a different direction.* It is from this viewpoint that we can discuss, indeed create, the promise of the twenty-first century, for promise there certainly is.

REVISITING THE THEMES OF THE BOOK

We began by sketching the magnitude of the changes now in train and suggesting that schools needed to respond to them. We examined the costs of the industrial way of life and suggested that some of the defects were a result of faulty programming in the Western world-view itself. We then considered the rise of globalism and the increasing interconnectedness of the world, suggesting that all education systems now needed to refer explicitly to this new, dynamic context.

With the costs and limitations of the standard industrial view in mind, we considered ways in which the world picture could be extended or changed in order to reflect what we have learned more recently about the way the world is made and how it functions. We showed how some very important features had been 'read out of the picture' and used an hierarchical metaphor to re-establish a broader and, in our view, a more promising outlook. From here we considered how educational organisation, language and metaphor might be modified to reflect this new (or renewed) world.

We identified the shift from past to future as pivotal for all of the above. It is the one single change which changes everything else. For once 'the future' is truly on the educational agenda, a whole host of other facilitative changes are that much easier to implement. Being mindful of the dangers of too much theorising, too much abstraction, we looked in some detail at a number of bridging strategies, ways of actually putting into practice some aspects of the new perspective. It has been our experience that the more these concepts, ideas, and strategies are used, the more productive they become. This reflects one of the key features of the human mind: once it focuses upon something, that 'something' grows and develops. That is why the focus of attention, and the nature of the human response to concerns, fears etc., are so crucial. So, when we take futures as the focus, we should not be surprised to find new ideas, projects, options and possibilities crowding into our attention. The challenging, open-ended nature of the subject is exactly what the human mind and spirit thrive upon. At some level we all know that it is this wider world which is primary, not the stifling prison of the instantaneous present which became dominant in the industrial view. Similarly, we also know that it is the perennial quest for meaning and significance, rather than power or possessions, which stirs us most profoundly. But the ego structure of the age blocks out these deeper satisfactions with a range of distractions (Wilber 1983: 13).

It is true that at first sight the notion of studying futures, of engaging with the challenges of present and future, or of developing a true futures pedagogy may seem daunting. But we cannot overemphasise, this is only a first view. We have each been responsible for teaching a range of futures-related courses in a number of countries. We have talked with many different people who found the ideas and perspectives challenging at first. But we have also had the pleasure of seeing what happens when they begin to find their feet and move with greater confidence in this exciting new field. So we, in turn, are confident that what we have tried to present in this book is not merely an academic exercise, not just theory. Anyone who cares to browse through the book and some of the rich literature cited in the bibliography will, we feel, find many sources of insight and inspiration, indeed, a deeper view of reality.

We hope that teachers will feel empowered to develop their own views of futures and then integrate these into every aspect of their work. For whether or not the twenty-first century turns out to be a renaissance or a continuing disaster depends, to no small extent, upon them.

THE CHALLENGE AND PROMISE OF THE 21ST CENTURY

Possible futures for humankind are many and varied. The inert, radioactive desert is still a possibility, though less likely than it once was. More likely now is a planet whose life-support systems are devastated beyond all hope of repair. In that scenario the four horsemen would ride at will across the densely-populated landscapes, wreaking their age-old havoc through famine, war, disease and pestilence. There are some who place their hope on 'the high frontier', namely the promise of space, orbiting colonies, mining

the asteroids and so on. As we have mentioned, others are un-
locking the DNA code, pursuing nanotechnology and other such
wonders. However, the flaw in many of these enterprises is that
they leave the question of human motives unaddressed.

It is our observation that when low-level human motives such as
fear, greed, and hostility become associated with powerful technologies, the result is indeed a long-running disaster. We have
seen many in recent history. But when higher motives such as
selfless love, stewardship and what Buddhists call 'loving kindness'
come into play, there are interesting consequences (Macy, 1991).
The grounds of many otherwise serious problems seem to disappear. Furthermore, many technologies are seen to be unavoid-
ably secondary. If they are applied at all, then it is sparingly. Ethical
concerns such as 'enoughness', a deep identification with the
natural world and a developed interest in future generations come
to the fore. In other words, when a right relationship is re-
established between people, culture and technology, a new world
of options emerges.

This does not mean going back to some pre-industrial condition
of innocence, for in many ways we have as a species needed the
twentieth century to make available to us certain kinds of experience, along with the experience of their costs and limitations. We
have learned that the assumptions about materialism, growth, the
world as a machine or a resource and so on are untenable. Con-
sequently, we are challenged to create a new synthesis, and that has
been the focus of this book.

The promise of the twenty-first century lies in our ability to
learn from the twentieth and collectively to decide to strike out in
a new or renewed direction (Milbrath, 1989). For us this means
giving up the disastrous conceits of the past and embarking on a
different journey to explore the heights, as opposed to the depths,
of human ability and potential. From that viewpoint the future
looks much less daunting. Powerful new technologies are not
intrinsically threatening. If they were linked to, and directed by, a
higher-order ethical commitment, they would be deployed in life-
affirming ways. For example, it need not be an expression of
hubris to imagine that we could re-invent some aspects of nature
and revive ravaged ecosystems. We may even be able to synthesise
the DNA of some extinct species and bring them back to life.
Speculative fiction is full of such seemingly improbable possib-

ilities. However, few of them make sense without the kinds of shifts we have outlined here.

To realise the potential of the twenty-first century we will need to put aside the obsessions of the 20th century, especially the fixation on what we may have, and return our attention to the perennial question of what we may be. That process can begin now, in schools. This book has been informed by the view that the outer world is an expression of the inner one. The biggest step forward would be re-establishing a map of culture which includes more than the material and the instrumental. We can then use the new map, the new world-view, both to frame and to define futures which breach the bounds of instrumental rationality and see human life as a self-aware part of the whole.

References

Albury, N. and Yule, V. (1989) *Encyclopedia of Social Inventions*, London: Institute for Social Inventions.

Andersen, U.S. (1954) *Three Magic Words*, North Hollywood, California: Wilshire Book Co.

Anderson, J. (ed.) (1987) *Shaping Education*, Carlton, Vic: Australian College of Education.

Anderson, W. (1987) *To Govern Evolution*, Orlando, Florida: Harcourt, Brace, Jovanovitoh.

Barr, T. (1988) 'Perspectives on Australia's Future' (Discussion Paper) Melbourne: Commission for the Future.

Bateson, G. (1979) *Mind and Nature: A Necessary Unity*, London: Wildwood House.

Beare, H. (1984) 'Education and the Post-industrial State', *Unicorn* 10(2), May.

Beare, H. (1987a) 'Metaphors about Schools: The Principal as a Cultural Leader' in Simpkins, W.S., Thomas, A.R. and Thomas, E.B. (eds) *The Principal and Change: The Australian Experience*, Armidale, New South Wales: University of New England Teaching Monograph Series.

Beare, H. (1987b) *Shared Meanings About Education: The Economic Paradigm Considered* (The Buntine Oration), Deakin, Australian Capital Territory: Australian College of Education.

Beare, H. and Millikan, R.H. (1988a) *Skilling the Australian Community: Futures for Public Education*, Carlton, Victoria: Commission for the Future and Australian Teachers Federation.

Beare, H. (1988b) 'School and System Management in Post-industrial Conditions', *Unicorn* 14(4), November.

Beare, H., Caldwell, B.J. and Millikan, R.H. (1989) *Creating an Excellent School: Some New Management Techniques*, London: Routledge.

Beare, H. (1989a) 'From "Educational Administration" to "Efficient Management": The New Metaphor in Australian Education in the 1980s'. Paper presented at the Annual Conference of the American Educational Research Association (AERA) in San Francisco, March 1989.

Beare, H. (1989b) *The Curriculum for the 1990s: A New Package or a New Spirit?* (The A.W. Jones Lecture), Occasional Paper No.12, Deakin, Australian Capital Territory: Australian College of Education.

Beare, H. (1990*a*) *Educational Administration in the 1990s* (ACEA Monograph No.6), Hawthorn, Victoria: Australian Council for Educational Administration.

Beare, H. (1990*b*) *An educator speaks to his grandchildren: some aspects of schooling in the new world context* (ACEA Monograph Series No.8), Hawthorn, Victoria: Australian Council for Educational Administration.

Bell, D. (1974) *The Coming of the Post-Industrial State*, London: Heinemann.

Bell, D. (1976) 'The Coming of the Post-industrial State', *Educational Forum* XL(4) May.

Belsey, C. (1980) *Critical Practice*, London: Methuen.

Benedict, R. (1935, 1961) *Patterns of Culture*, London: Routledge and Kegan Paul.

Berman, M. (1981) *The Re-enchantment of the World*, Hartford, Conn.: Cornell University Press.

Berman, M. (1990) *Coming to Our Senses*, New York: Bantam Books.

Berry, T. (1988) *The Dream of the Earth*, San Francisco: Sierra Club.

Bohm, D. (1980) *Wholeness and the Implicate Order*, London: Routledge and Kegan Paul.

Bohm, D. (1985) *Unfolding Meaning*, London: Routledge and Kegan Paul.

Boulding, E. (1988) 'Image and Action in Peace Building', *Journal of Social Issues* 44(2), 17–37.

Briggs, J. and Peat, D. (1984) *Looking Glass Universe: The Emerging Science of Wholeness*, New York: Simon and Schuster.

Broms, H. and Gahmberg, H. (1983) 'Communication to Self in Organisations and Culture', *Administrative Science Quarterly*, September 1983, 482–95.

Brown, H. (1986) *The Wisdom of Science: Its Relevance to Culture and Religion*, Cambridge: Cambridge University Press.

Brown, L. (*et al.*) 1991 *The State of the World 1991*, New York: Worldwatch Institute/Allen and Unwin.

(Brundtland Report) (1988) World Commission on Environment and Development (United Nations). *Our Common Future*, Oxford: Oxford University Press.

Burdin, J.L. (ed.) (1989) *School Leadership: A Contemporary Reader*, Newbury Park, California: Sage Publications.

Burrell, G. and Morgan, G. (1980) *Sociological Paradigms and Organizational Analysis*, London: Heinemann.

Busuttil, S. (*et al.*) (1990) *Our Responsibilities to Future Generations*, Malta: Foundation for International Studies.

Campbell, J. (1972) *Myths To Live By*, London: Paladin.

Campbell, J. (1973) *The Masks of God*, London: Paladin.

Campbell, J. (1988a) *The Hero with a Thousand Faces*, London: Paladin.

Campbell, J. (1988b) *The Inner Reaches of Outer Space*, New York: Harper & Row.

Capra, F. (1975) *The Tao of Physics*, London: Wildwood House.

Capra, F. (1982) *The Turning Point: Science, Society and The Rising Culture*, London: Fontana Paperbacks.

Carretto, C. (1975) *In Search of the Beyond*, London: Darton Longman and Todd.

Chetwynd, T. (1982) *A Dictionary of Symbols*, London: Granada.

Clark, D.L., Lotto, L.S., and Astuto, T.A. (1989) 'Effective Schools and School Improvement: A Comparative Analysis of Two Lines of Inquiry' in Burdin, J.L.

Clarke, I.F. (1979) *The Pattern of Expectation 1644–2001*, London: Jonathan Cape.

Davies, P. (1983) *God and the New Physics*, Harmondsworth, Middlesex: Pelican.

Davies, P. (1991) *The Mind of God*, New York: Simon and Schuster.

Deal, T.E. and Kennedy, A.A. (1982) *Corporate Cultures: The Rites and Rituals of Corporate Life*. Reading, Mass.: Addison-Wesley.

Devall, B. and Sessions, G. (1985) *Deep Ecology: Living as if Nature Mattered*, Salt Lake City, Peregrine Smith Books.

Dossey, L. (1982) *Space, Time and Medicine*, Boulder, Colorado and London: Shambhala.

Drexler, K.E. (1986) *Engines of Creation: The Coming Era of Nanotechnology*, New York: Anchor Books (Doubleday).

Dyson, F. (1981) *Disturbing the Universe*, London: Pan Books.

Ellul, J. (1990) *The Technological Bluff*, Grand Rapids, Michigan: Wm. B. Ferdmans Pub. Co.

Elgin, D. (1981) *Voluntary Simplicity: Towards a Way of Life that is Outwardly Simple, Inwardly Rich*, New York: William Morrow and Co.

Ferguson, M. (1980) *The Aquarian Conspiracy: Personal and Social Transformation in the 1980s*, Los Angeles: J.P. Tarchar, Inc.

Fischer, K.R. (1983) *The Inner Rainbow: The Imagination in the Christian Life*, New York: Paulist Press.

Fisher, F. (1987) 'Ways of knowing and the ecology of change'. Proceedings of *Barriers to Change*. UNESCO Network for Appropriate Technology, University of Melbourne, 11–16 November.

Fitch, R. and Svengalis, C. (1979) *Futures Unlimited: Teaching About Worlds to Come*, Washington D.C.: National Council for the Social Studies.

Fox, M. (1983) *Original Blessings*, Santa Fe, New Mexico: Bear and Co.

Frankl, V. (1959, 1984) *Man's Search for Meaning*, New York: Simon and Schuster.

Fraser, J.T. (1978) *Time as Conflict*, Basle, Birk Hauser Verl Ag.

Fraser, J.T. (1987) *Time the Familiar Stranger*, Washington: Microsoft.

Gerding, G., and Serenhuijsen, R.F. (1987) 'Public Managers in the Middle' in Kooiman and Eliassen.

Glassman, R.B. (1973) 'Persistence and Loose Coupling in Living Systems', *Behavioral Science*, vol. 18, 83–98.

Goldberg, P. (1983) *The Intuitive Edge*, Los Angeles: J.P. Tarcher Inc.

Gough, N. (1985, 1990) *Some Australian Initiatives in Futures Education: Project If and Other Stories*, Melbourne: Victoria College.

Grumet, M.(1981) 'Restitution and Reconstruction of Educational Experience' in *Rethinking Curriculum Studies*, Lawn, M. and Barton, L. (eds), London: Croom Helm.

Habermas, J. (1971) *Towards a Rational Society*, London: Heinemann.

Handy, C.B. (1978) *Gods of Management*, London: Pan Books.

Handy, C.B. (1985) *Understanding Organisations*, 3rd ed.,

Harmondsworth, Middlesex: Penguin.

Handy, C.B. and Aitken, R. (1986) *Understanding Schools as Organisations*, Harmondsworth, Middlesex: Penguin.

Handy, C.B. (1989) *The Age of Unreason*, London: Century Hutchinson.

Harman, G., Beare, H. and Berkley, F. (1991) *Restructuring School Management*, Curtin, A.C.T., Australian College of Education.

Harman, W. (1988) *Global Mind Change: The Promise of the Last Years of the Twentieth Century*, Indianapolis: Knowledge Systems Inc.

Harner, M. (1990) *The Way of The Shaman*, 3rd ed., New York: Harper and Row.

Hayes, R. and Watts, R. (1986) *Corporate Revolution: New Strategies for Executive Leadership*, London: Heinemann.

Henderson, H. (1978) *Creating Alternative Futures*, New York: Berkley Books.

Henderson, H. (1981) *The Politics of the Solar Age*, New York: Anchor Books/Doubleday.

Henderson, R. (1983) 'The folly of job creation without job planning', *Australian Society*, July 1.

Hesse, H. (1951) *Siddhartha*, New York: New Directions Pubs.

Hicks, P. (ed.) (1988) *Education for Peace: Issues, Principles and Practice in the Classroom*, London: Routledge.

Hirshchorn, L. (1979) 'Post-Industrial Life: A U.S. Perspective', *Futures*, August.

House of Representatives Standing Committee for Long Term Strategies (1991) *Australia as an Information Society*, Canberra: Government Printing Office.

Huxley, A. (1945) *The Perennial Philosophy*, London: Chatto and Windus.

Jones, B. (1982, revised 1989) *Sleepers Wake! Technology and the Future of Work*, Melbourne: Oxford University Press.

Jouvenal, B. de (1967) *The Art of Conjecture*, London: Weidenfeld and Nicholson.

Kauffman, D. (1976) *Teaching the Future*, Palm Springs, California: ETC Pubs.

Kooiman, J. and Eliassen, K.A. (eds) (1987) *Managing Public Organisations: Lessons from Contemporary European Experience*, London: Sage.

Koprowski, E.J. (1983) 'Cultural Myths: Clues to Effective Management', *Organisational Dynamics*, Autumn 1983, 39–51.

Kovel, J. (1983) *Against the State of Nuclear Terror*, London: Pan Books/Channel Four.

Kuhn, T.S. (1962) *The Structure of Scientific Revolutions*, Chicago: University of Chicago Press.

Lasch, C. (1985) *The Minimal Self*, London: Picador.

Laughlin, C. and Richardson, R. (1986) 'The Future of Human Consciousness,' *Futures*, 17(3), 401–19.

Lawn, M. and Barton, L. (eds) (1981) *Rethinking Curriculum Studies*, London: Croom Helm.

Le Guin, U. (1985) *Always Coming Home*, New York: Harper and Row.

Leiss, W. (1976) *The Limits to Satisfaction*, Toronto: University of Toronto Press.

Lefanu, S. (1988) *In the Chinks of the World Machine*, London: Women's Press.

Lovelock, J. (1979) *Gaia: A New Look at Life on Earth*, London: Oxford University Press.

Lovelock, J. (1988) *The Ages of Gaia: A Biography of Our Living Earth*, London: Oxford University Press.

Macini, E. (ed.) (1983) *Visions of Desirable Societies*, Oxford: Pergamon.

Macy, J. (1983) 'Despair and Personal Power' in *The Nuclear Age*, Philadelphia: New Society Pubs.

Macy, J. (1991) *World as Lover, World as Self*, Berkeley, California: Parallax Press.

McClendon, J. (1974) *Biography as Theology*, New York: Abingdon Press.

McDonagh, S. (1986) *To Care for the Earth: A Call to a New Theology*, London: Geoffrey Chapman.

Merton, R.K. (1973) *The Sociology of Science*, Chicago: Chicago University Press.

Milbrath, L. (1989) *Envisioning a Sustainable Society*, New York: Suny Press.

Moltmann, J. (1989) *Creating a Just Future: The Politics of Peace and the Ethics of Creation in a Threatened World*, London: SCM Press.

Morgan, G. (1980) 'Paradigms, Metaphors, and Puzzle Solving in Organisation Theory'. *Administrative Science Quarterly*.

Muller, R. (1979) *New Genesis: Shaping a Global Spirituality*, New York: Doubleday.

Mumford, L. (1971) *The Pentagon of Power*, London: Weidenfeld and Nicolson.

Naess, A. (1986) 'An Ecological Approach to Being in the World', the 1986 Roby Memorial Lecture, Murdoch University, Perth, Western Australia.

Naisbitt, J. (1982) *Megatrends: Ten New Directions Transforming Our Lives*, New York: Warren Books.

Naisbitt, J. and Aburdene, P. (1986) *Re-Inventing the Corporation: Transforming your job and your company for the new information society*, London: Macdonald and Co.

Neville, B. (1989) (reprinted 1992) *Educating Psyche: Emotion, Imagination and the Unconscious in Learning*, Melbourne: Collins Dove.

Noyce, P. (ed.) (1987) *Futures in Education: The Report*, Melbourne: Commission for the Future.

Otto, R. (1923) *The Idea of The Holy*, Oxford: Oxford University Press.

Page, C. (1986) 'Service Industries Setting the Pace', *National Times on Sunday*, 14 December.

Pannikar, R. (ed.) (1982) *Blessed Simplicity: The Monk as Universal Archetype*, New York: Seabury Press.

Peat, F.D. (1987) *Synchronicity: The Bridge between Matter and Mind*, London: Bantam Books.

Peters, T.J. and Waterman, R.H. (1982) *In Search of Excellence*, New York: Bantam Books.

Popper, K. (1988) Transcript from World Congress of Philosophy Address, Brighton, UK.

Postman, N. (1986) *Amusing Ourselves to Death*, London: Methuen.

Pusey, M. (1991) *Economic Rationalism in Canberra: A Nation-Building State Changes Its Mind*, Melbourne: Cambridge University Press.

Reanney, D. (1991) *The Death of Forever*, Melbourne: Longman Cheshire.

Roszak, T. (1978) *Person–Planet: The Creative Disintegration of Industrial Society*, New York: Anchor Books (Doubleday).

Saaty, T.L. and Boone, L.W. (1990) *Embracing the Future: Meeting the Challenge of Our Changing World*, New York: Praeger Publishers.

Schell, J. (1982) *The Fate of the Earth*, London: Picador.

Schon, D. (1971) *Beyond the Stable State*, London: Temple Smith.

Schumacher, E.F. (1977) *Guide for the Perphexed*, London: Jonathan Cape.

Sheldrake, R. (1981) *A New Science of Life: The Hypothesis of Formative Causation*, London: Blond & Briggs.

Simpkins, W.S., Thomas, A.R., and Thomas, E.B. (eds) (1987) *The Principal and Change: The Australian Experience*, Armidale, New South Wales: University of New England Teaching Monograph Series.

Skilbeck, M. (ed.) (1984) *Readings in School-Based Curriculum Development*, London: Harper and Row.

Slaughter, R. (1984) 'Futures Study in the Curriculum' in Skilbeck 290–304.

Slaughter, R. (1985) 'The Dinosaur and the Dream: Re-thinking Education for the Future'. *World Studies Journal* 6 (1) 2–6.

Slaughter, R. (1987*a*) 'Future Vision in the Nuclear Age,' *Futures*, 19(1), 54–72.

Slaughter, R. (1987*b*) 'Futures in Education: A Human Agenda', in Noyce, P., 13–26.

Slaughter, R. (1987*c*) *Futures Tools and Techniques*, Melbourne: Futures Study Centre.

Slaughter, R. (1988) *Recovering the Future*, Melbourne: Graduate School of Environment Science, Monash University.

Slaughter, R. (ed.) (1989*a*) *Studying the Future*, Melbourne: Commission for the Future.

Slaughter, R. (1989*b*) 'Cultural re-construction in the Post-modern Age', *Journal of Curriculum Studies*, 21(3), 255–70.

Slaughter, R. (1990*a*) 'Assessing the Quest for Future Knowledge', *Futures* 22(2), 153–66.

Slaughter, R. (1990*b*) 'The Foresight Principle', *Futures*, 22(8), 801–19.

Slaughter, R. (1991*a*) *Futures Concepts and Powerful Ideas*, Melbourne: Futures Study Centre.

Slaughter, R. (1991*b*) 'The Machine at the Heart of the World: Technology, Violence and Futures in Young People's Media', *Papers: Explorations in Children's Literature* 2(1), 3–23.

Slaughter, R. (1991*c*) 'Changing Images of Futures in the 20th Century', *Futures* 23(5), 499–515.

Stableford, B. and Langford, D. (1985) *The Third Milennium: A History of the World: AD 2000–3000*, London: Sidgewick and Jackson.

Swimme, B. (1984) *The Universe is a Green Dragon: The Cosmic Creation Story*, Santa Fe: Bear and Co.

Teilhard De Chardin, P. (1961) *The Phenomenon of Man*, London: Harper Torchbooks.

Teilhard De Chardin, P. (1961) *Hymn of the Universe*, London: Fontana Books.

Toffler, A. (ed.) (1974) *Learning for Tomorrow: The Role of the Future in Education*, New York: Vintage Books/Random House.

Toffler, A. (1985) *The Adaptive Corporation*, London: Pan Books.

Tough, A. (1991) *Crucial Questions About the Future*, Lanham, Maryland: University Press of America.

Tydeman, J. (1987) *Futures Methodology Handbook*, Melbourne: Commission for the Future.

Underhill, E. (1955) *Mysticism: A Study in the nature and development of Man's Spiritual Consciousness*, New York: Meridian Books (first published, 1911).

Weber, R. (1983) *Dialogues With Scientists and Sages: The Search for Unity*, London: Routledge and Kegan Paul.

Webster, F. and Lambe, K. (1986) 'Information Technology – Who needs it?' in Weston, J.

Weston, J. (ed.) (1986) *Red and Green, The New Politics of the Environment*, London: Pluto Press.

Weick, K. (1976) 'Educational Organisations as Loosely Coupled Systems', *Administrative Science Quarterly*, vol.21, March, 1–19.

Wilber, K. (1979) *No Boundary*, Boulder, Colorado: Shambhala Publications.

Wilber, K. (1983) *Eye to Eye: The Quest for The New Paradigm*, Garden City, New York: Anchor Books (Doubleday).

Wilber, K. (ed.) (1984) *Quantum Questions: Mystical Writings of the World's Great Physicists*, Boulder, Colorado: Shambhala Publications.

Woodcock, A. and Davis, M. (1978) *Catastrophe Theory*, Harmondsworth, Middlesex: Penguin.

Index